C.P.R.R.
OAKLAND, ALAMEDA & BERKELEY
FERRY.
SACRAMENTO.
LOS ANGELES.
CHICAGO.
NEW YORK.
STATION "D" POST OFFICE.
GRAND CREDIT AUCTION SALE OF
BERKELEY
AT AUCTION
VALENCIA 11th STREET

SAN FRANCISCO AS IT IS AS IT WAS

SAN FRANCISCO AS IT IS AS IT WAS

by Paul C. Johnson and Richard Reinhardt

Foreword by Herb Caen

with contemporary photographs by Suellen Bilow-Lerch Kurt Reinhardt Norman Prince, and many others

Doubleday & Company, Inc., Garden City, New York 1979

On a misty morning in the 1880s a boy named Louis Slevin sits with his father on the jetsam-strewn beach of the Presidio, gazing at Alcatraz Island and the bay.

Library of Congress Cataloging in Publication Data

Johnson, Paul C 1910–76
San Francisco—as it is, as it was.

Includes index.
1. San Francisco—History. 2. San Francisco—Description. I. Reinhardt, Richard, joint author.
II. Title.
F869.S357J64 979.4'61

ISBN: 0-385-09882-0
Library of Congress Catalog Card Number 77-80891

Printed in the United States of America
First edition

On an afternoon in the 1970s a father and son, ignoring distractions, give preflight attention to a kite while one of the Marina's myriad joggers bounces past.

Contents

Stripped for action, a coeducational bathing party pranced around a water jet in Haig Patigian's Wind and Spray, *an embellishment of the Palace of Fine Arts at the Panama-Pacific International Exposition in 1915.*

Caves and catwalks lead viewers under the tumbling cascades of Armand Vaillancourt's angular Embarcadero Fountain (1971) at the foot of Market Street. Former Mayor Joseph Alioto, whose administration commissioned the work, called it "more beautiful than the Spanish Steps in Rome," while an unidentified observer has likened it to "the tailings of a giant, concrete-eating, square-bottomed worm."

The Grand Court of the Palace Hotel, seven stories high and crowned with frosted glass, set a world standard of splendor from 1875 to 1906. Atrium lobby of Hyatt Regency (right), built in 1973, rises seventeen stories, engulfing a hundred full-grown trees, five restaurants, Charles O. Perry's forty-foot sculpture Eclipse, *and innumerable conventioneers. It could have gobbled up the Grand Court of the Palace, too, but that succumbed to the earthquake-fire.*

Above: The City That Was, viewed northward along Kearny Street from the top floor of the Spreckels Building at Third and Market Streets on a morning in 1905, a few months before fire and earthquake leveled the downtown area. Among the few structures that have survived are the de Young Building (clock tower at lower right, now the much-remodeled American Savings visible on the opposite page), the Mills Building (center right), and the spire from which the picture was taken (now the Central Tower). Right: The City That Is, from the same vantage point seventy-three years later. The massive bronzed post pile of the Bank of America Building rules the scene, blocking all but a glimpse of Telegraph Hill. The street pattern alone is unchanged.

CHARLESTON BUILDING
Santa Barbara Savings

Telegraph Hill in the 1890s provided a raw brown pedestal for the crenellated German Castle observatory-restaurant at Kearny and Greenwich Streets. At center is Dupont Street (Grant Avenue), at right, Stockton Street.

A Web of Memories and Dreams

by Herb Caen

Are any people more obsessed with the past (and future) of their own city than San Franciscans? Almost daily, it seems, we scrabble through the shards and artifacts of this small place, looking for reassurance that we are the inheritors of a grand tradition, worrying the while that we are not doing all we might to keep the flame alive.

It is such a young city to be so tradition-obsessed, and yet it is unarguable that San Franciscans live more deeply in the past than in the present. That such nostalgia borders on the neurotic will not be denied except by the most unimaginative. We are still puzzled and fascinated that the city became world-famous overnight, and we want to "see" it now as the great world saw it then. If there was a special magic—and the testimony of writers from Mark Twain to Oscar Wilde, from Robert Louis Stevenson to Rudyard Kipling says there was indeed—we long to reassure ourselves, and be reassured, that it is still here, strong and flourishing.

Like troubled souls, adrift in a strange new world, we pore over sepia photographs and walk along old and unchanged side streets, as though seeking signals from yesterday. We look at the pioneer faces and know they were a different breed,

Viewed from a harbor tour boat in the late 1970s, the familiar outline remains, but downtown towers—the spindly Transamerica, the craggy Bank of America—loom to the south, dwarfing the 274-foot hill.

those early San Franciscans. We read their words and marvel at their confidence. We stare, long minutes at a time, at the grand buildings they left behind—the pitiful few that have survived—and wonder at their matter-of-fact magnificence. Our forebears seem to have been free of doubt, utterly convinced that they had found their roots in a great city and would leave it even greater.

It is a hopeless cliché now to say, "San Francisco isn't what it used to be," and of course it isn't. The memory plays tricks, and perhaps we are looking back with an overly selective eye, seeing only the glories, glossing over the poverty and seaminess, the undoubted bawdiness and depravity of the Barbary Coast, the sometimes inhuman treatment of the Orientals, the political knavery and connivance.

But we do know there was a tremendous vitality then, expressed in mansions more lavish than any others west of Chicago, in lacy ferryboats, careening cable cars, and restaurants of undoubted variety and quality. That kind of vitality reaches across the decades to the present. Many a precious old building has gone, true, but many a remarkable new one has risen, and the streets are teeming with the most diverse parade of "types" and "characters"—San Francisco has always had a fondness for "characters"—to be seen anywhere in the world.

In fact, as big cities become more and more homogenized, San Francisco stands out even more sharply as one of the few that are still "different." In this small and precious corner of the world, it is still possible to live as you wish, dress as you please, and go about your business in a civilized manner—that is, without making an undue fuss and bothering others who may wish to go THEIR way.

Most world cities measure their lives in centuries. San Francisco's seems to be a matter of decades, each one strikingly different. From Gold Rush to Bonanza Kings, from the Naughty Nineties to the Roaring Twenties (our speakeasies were incomparable), from the war years to Beats of the 1950s, the hippies of the 1960s, the relative sophisticated calm of the 1970s—the city remains remarkably vital and open to even more change.

This book spins its own web of memories and dreams, desperation and reality. It is one more piece of compelling evidence that San Franciscans—and San Francisco-lovers—will never tire of examining and probing their city, always aware that all the tantalizing questions can never be answered. Who would want it any other way?

Above: Downtown San Francisco and the northern waterfront in 1955.

Below: The same view, from a lower elevation, twenty years later.

CHAPTER 1

The Urge to Grow

Most cities have Rip Van Winkle places—neighborhoods through which one wanders in a state of shock, fighting an irrational impression that one has been sleeping for twenty years.

In San Francisco it is the downtown center, the heart of the city, that has changed so unbelievably in the last two decades. Urban renewal, real estate speculation, and a peculiar form of civic pride that equates growth with success all have contributed to the transformation of a modest, pastel skyline into a dark and bristling battlement of corporate castles.

Gone are the produce sheds of lower Washington Street, the red brick basements where regiments of green bananas ripened in clouds of sulfur dioxide. Gone are the ship chandleries and stand-up bars, the trolley turnabouts and sailors' rooms of lower Market Street. Gone (or, rather, *scattered,*) are the gray saloons and bottle-in-a-bag shops of Skid Row; the drop-in political offices and discount shoe stores of Fifth and Market; the bail bond brokerages of Portsmouth Square.

Everything nowadays is pedestrian malls and miniparks and Indian fig laurel trees in concrete tubs. Fountains splash above the air vents where the transit trains go slithering away to Walnut Creek and Daly City. Great totem poles of polished wood and burnished metal whistle in the wind that slices among the towers.

Searching in vain for landmarks, Rip Van Winkle seizes with delight on any object out of the past: only let the blessed thing be well worn, hand-rubbed, time-stained, and aboriginal. Thus it is that enterprising caterers sandblast the masonry of loft warehouses in the alleys off Mission Street and offer bean sprout sandwiches and carrot cake under the monumental shade of Standard Oil. Strange old statues, excesses of the 1890s, are raised on pedestals beside the unquiet boulevards. Hirsute young violinists play Mozart and Vivaldi on the corners of Grant Avenue. And street merchants sell hand-tooled leather and used denim trousers under all the shining new façades.

1910—The 235-foot Ferry Building stands out with architectural hubris in this gull's-eye view of the downtown waterfront. The bulky white structure on Nob Hill is the Fairmont Hotel.

An Uprising by the Bay

A real estate developer from the East, visiting San Francisco in the early 1950s, rubbed his hands together and said, "San Francisco could be the New York of this generation."

Although nobody knew precisely what he had in mind, it sounded exciting, not to say aggrandizing, and stirred up visions of opening nights on Broadway, ticker-tape parades, the ice rink in Rockefeller Center, and tall, very tall buildings.

Not everyone was enchanted. To the contrary, no other question of municipal development except automobile freeways ever has so deeply divided the city. The Chamber of Commerce, predictably, poured out reports assuring the public that taller office buildings, apartment houses, and hotels would make the city healthy, wealthy, and beautiful. The opposition, in full-page newspaper advertisements signed by Alvin Duskin, a dress manufacturer who became the self-appointed leader of an anti-high-rise campaign, mourned, "Soon, this last liveable American city will look and feel like [Chicago and New York]—airless, viewless, crowded, dirty, noisy, smelly, dangerous, and expensive."

That neither view was fully justified is evidenced here and in succeeding pages. In any case, the argument is futile, for there is every indication that high-rise building will continue through the 1980s, adding to the city as much office space as four dozen new Transamerica Pyramids.

Viewed from Russian Hill in 1930, the titans of the skyline are the thirty-one-story Russ Building (center), three years old and tallest in the West; the thirty-story Shell Building (left); and the twenty-six-story Pacific Telephone Building (right).

1975—New lords of the downtown sky are the 853-foot Transamerica Pyramid (far right) and the dark tower of the Bank of America (778 feet tall, 52 stories). The Ferry Building, humbled by upstart neighbors, is visible where Market Street forms a gap in the rampart of buildings.

Topping-off ceremonies brought a brass band in hard hats to Montgomery Street in June 1965. At forty-three stories, the new Wells Fargo Building seemed (and was) a big spike, but there were bigger ones to come.

The view from Russian Hill, 1975, is crowned by the bulwark of the Bank of America. The Russ Building has disappeared from view; the Shell Building seems to shrink in shame. Holding its own in the foreground is the twin-spired church of Nuestra Señora de Guadalupe.

A Century Along the Slot

An Irishman named Jasper O'Farrell laid out the metes and bounds of Market Street, and Philadelphia contributed the name. Aside from these foreign influences, Market Street always has been an obstinately original thoroughfare.

For one thing, it runs at a slant to the rest of the downtown district, forming a three-mile-long, 120-foot-wide diagonal from the Ferry Building to the foot of Twin Peaks, where it climbs in sinuous splendor to the summit of the city. If this sounds pretentious, that is exactly what Market Street was meant to be—an imperial boulevard, appropriate to ceremonial processions and triumphal marches.

Thousands of parades have indeed rolled along these pavements. Betweentimes, ordinary folk have taken over, marking the great concourse with our taste for hot dogs, chewing gum, pink neon, and cheap shoes. The result is an imposing but earthy boulevard, livelier than it is beautiful. When cable car promoters dug a groove along the center in the 1880s, the vulgar masses nicknamed it "The Slot." Who can make grandeur out of that?

Mechanics Monument, Douglas Tilden's statue of muscular ironworkers struggling with an antique punch press, was surrounded by a reflecting pool and low Italianate buildings in the 1890s. Now the center of a wedge-shaped mini-park, the monument at Bush and Sansome is a noontime rendezvous for office workers who pay little attention to it.

Left: Marble works, bookstores, and bars lined the plank sidewalks in 1865, just eighteen years after O'Farrell laid out the street. Right: Same street, southwest from Montgomery Street, shows new brick sidewalks and plane trees after its $35 million beautification in the 1970s.

Busy corner of Ellis and Market on a rainy day in 1883 was jammed with horse-drawn trolleys, beer wagons, and one stray dog.

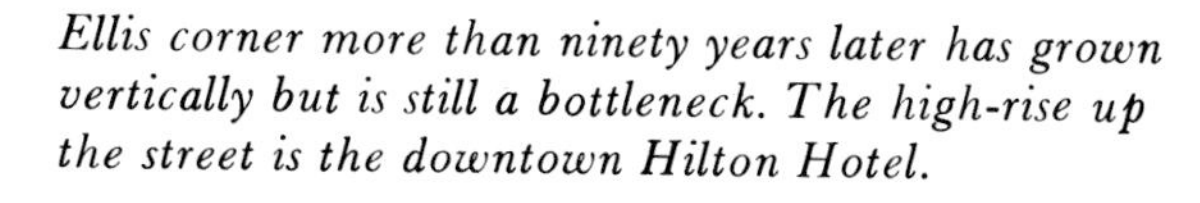

Ellis corner more than ninety years later has grown vertically but is still a bottleneck. The high-rise up the street is the downtown Hilton Hotel.

The Coming of Age of Market Street

For its first hundred years, Market Street rejoiced in the uncritical devotion of its patrons. Most San Franciscans were proud to have a main street that was wide and straight, well-paved and prosperous, although it was neither handsome nor efficient. When the earthquake and fire of 1906 ruined hundreds of downtown blocks, property owners rebuilt Market Street more or less the way it was before.

After World War II, however, when traffic congealed and downtown shoppers defected to the suburbs, city planners and merchant associations discovered a subversive influence right in the heart of the city: it was none other than Market Street, the splendid main stem! Not only did The Slot *look* seedy, it was a Barrier to Progress, preventing the free flow of automobiles between the retail districts to the north and the broad, flat blocks to the south, where corporations hankered to construct new office towers.

The upshot of this revelation was a municipal program to "transform the dreary arterial into a magnificent linear boulevard," as a citizens' committee phrased it in 1968—new cross-streets, plazas, benches, landscapes, and an end to all those jutting signs.

That Market Street looks better cannot be denied. What is surprising is that it looks so much the same—neither a truly dreary arterial nor a magnificent linear boulevard, but, as always, a little of both.

Survivor of earthquake and fire, the prow-shaped Flood Building at Powell and Market towered over rubble and temporary shops in 1906 (top) and over penny arcades and third-run movie houses in the late 1950s (center). Removal of a block of stores in the 1970s to create Hallidie Plaza revealed an architectural kinship between the Flood Building and a white granite branch office of the Bank of America, but the resulting plaza—a brash and breezy crossroad of tourists, commuters, peddlers, and panhandlers—is considerably less dignified than structures around it.

A sunny afternoon in the 1890s lures well-dressed strollers to the north side of Market Street near Grant Avenue. The domed edifice down the way is the Call Building, gutted by fire in 1906.

Same view eastward from Grant Avenue eighty years later. The Call Building, reconstructed and stripped of ornament, is now the Central Tower. Cast-iron lampposts, plane trees, and brick pavements impart a latter-day grace, and the strollers (mostly) have abandoned hats.

In a sunken plaza at the Powell-Market transit station, torch-tossing jugglers attract the mild interest of midday idlers.

Bench warmers on Hallidie Plaza enjoy continuous entertainment: sidewalk evangelists, street musicians, families boarding cable cars, commuters riding up and down the escalators.

The Tender Twig

If Market Street is the main stem, Powell is its flashiest branch—not the prettiest, not the cleanest, but the most conspicuous. Before Prohibition turned off the lights and sent everyone around to the side door, the Techau Tavern—"San Francisco's Leading High-Class Family Cafe"—used to hand out gifts of face powder and lilac perfume to ladies who showed up for what was discreetly advertised as "tea dancing." The Portola-Louvre, across the street, served thousands of two-dollar dinners on nights before the Cal-Stanford Big Game. And Newman's College Inn—ah! That was where you got an enchilada and a free lunch with a ten-cent beer. A bit pricey, people said.

They called the area the "Uptown Tenderloin." Around the corner were the Orpheum, the Tivoli, the Heidelberg, and the Tait-Zinkand cabaret, with an upstairs dance floor called Tait's Pavo Real. Up the street, Tessie Wall's parlor: red plush, ormolu, and gilded mirrors.

It's still the Tenderloin, but without the sentiment that mists the memories. That drunk collapsing in a doorway is a decoy cop. The blonde at the corner is a boy in drag. Newman's ran out of free enchiladas sixty years ago. The bill of fare along the cable line is frozen yogurt, chili dogs, and Wild Turkey on-the-rocks.

Lower Powell Street in the late 1920s had a quiet dignity, imposed upon it by the Dries, but old-timers could tell you that the Pig 'n' Whistle Restaurant was no substitute for the Techau, nor a Frank Werner shoe store for the Portola-Louvre. Fifty years later (below) sightseers line up to board a cable car, Werner's is a Woolworth store, and the Edison Theatre has gone to the projection room in the sky.

Glowing in anticipation of a spending spree, bars and cafes at Powell and Eddy greeted a convention of Native Sons of the Golden West on an evening just after World War I (above). Although Powell still lights up at dusk, most of the bartenders and dancing girls have taken their blenders and their sequins and moved a few blocks west, into a less tender loin.

TECHAU
TAVERN
NEWMAN
TECHAU TAVERN
CALIFORNIA
CAFE
HOTEL

LAMBO'S
LAMBO'S
FAMOUS
YOGURT
BAR
Try Our
Coffee...
It's the best
in Town"
Marinello
PUB

North of California Street in 1905, "The Street" has a mellow Germanic dignity. The same blocks in 1977 are dominated by the bulky Security Pacific Building and the tapering Transamerica. The Renaissance-style Kohi Building on the northeast corner served as headquarters for military officers directing fire fighters in 1906.

Of Time and Money

There was a time, as every child in San Francisco learns, when the waters of the bay lapped at the back doors of business houses on the east side of Montgomery Street. Merchants came and went like Venetian doges, racing each other in whaleboats to meet the latest clippers from the East.

"The early bird was eminently successful in those days," old William Coleman recalled in the 1880s, counting up the fortune he had made with advance information semaphored to his private telegraph station by incoming ships.

From the days of barter to those of option trading, Montgomery has remained a street of brokers and bankers—a street, in other words, where time and money are synonymous. Three thousand miles from Wall Street: three extra hours each day to buy and sell! Timing is all . . . When to buy shares in the Comstock bonanza, and when quietly to short-sell your partners . . . When to buy the bank across the street, and when to dump the raisin crop . . . When to ship a gold dredge to the Yukon . . . When to pull the plug on City Hall . . . When to yield and when to shove . . .

Computers, telephones, and photocopying machines have a place on every business street. The device that rules Montgomery Street is the clock.

Clocking in at the Crocker-First National Bank in March 1935, everyone from president to janitor set his watch by a new timepiece in the floor which kept banker's hours.

According to stock market theorists, Tucker's Clock, gleaming from a Gothic tower at Bush and Montgomery in the 1880s, regulated the movement of the sun. Right: In this contemporary scene, the Palace Hotel, substantially rebuilt after the quake, still stands on the other side of Market Street, but Tucker's Clock is gone, suggesting a downside technical adjustment in the normal diurnal behavior of the sun—or perhaps the need of a new theory.

Three Financiers who Shaped the City

Gold rush banker William Tecumseh Sherman (left) ran Bank of Lucas, Turner. A decade later he became a Union general. Bonanza banker William C. Ralston (center) led a ring of speculators who plundered Nevada's silver mines in the 1860s and '70s, built hotels, theaters, factories. Branch banker A. P. Giannini (right) founded Bank of America on loans, services to small businesses and farmers.

Closing hour on the floor of the San Francisco Stock Exchange (now the Pacific Stock Exchange) on an afternoon in 1946 found dealers checking order books, lighting cigarettes, reading over the day's highs and lows.

Stock board in a basement tavern kept customers posted on prices of Nevada mining shares in 1884. A London newspaper, reflecting British views of the Wild West, labeled the scene "an underground drinking cellar."

Women in uniform chalked up highs and lows in the boardroom of a brokerage on Post Street thirty years ago. Hats and blackboards have succumbed to changing fashion (as has this venerable stock and bond house), but customers still gather in some brokers' offices to follow movements of the market on electronic screens.

Ups and Downs in the Bear Garden

When the San Francisco Stock Exchange merged with the Los Angeles Exchange in 1957 there was dark keening here by the bay.

What had happened to the Wall Street of the West? Were we now to be enslaved not only to New York but also to the unspeakable Southern Californians? To those of us who judge economic activity by the volume of frenzy on a trading floor, it seemed that a century of struggle for local autonomy had ended in defeat.

Gold rush San Francisco was a colonial outpost, governed and manipulated from the East. Within a decade, thanks to the discovery of silver in Nevada, the city became a major stock market with a board that did more business on feverish days than the New York Exchange. The bell announcing a call for bids would set off a pandemonium of shrieks and howls. Sidewalk traders and fanatical women speculators known as "mudhens" jammed the surrounding streets so tightly that brokers had to be escorted in and out by squads of policemen. For the few who made and kept fortunes—Jim Keene, "Lucky" Baldwin, William Sharon, and the like—it truly was an age of gold.

Now that our local market is merely a unit in the Pacific Stock Exchange and our Mining Exchange has closed its doors, however, we have discovered that it is not necessary to have a private market place in order to buy and sell, win and lose. In an age of computer terminals and telex messages, one Wall Street is quite enough, and it seems profitless, indeed, to mourn the passing of bull markets in penny mining stocks on Leidesdorff Street.

"I certainly never saw such a bear garden among businessmen," an English visitor wrote after a visit to the San Francisco Stock and Exchange Board in 1878. "The chairman sounds an electric bell; someone shouts out the name of a stock; up spring a certain number of broadcloth-covered gentlemen, who rush into the arena and commence a free fight . . . They push one another about, shout at the top of their voices, set upon one man like the canine species when one has seized a bone, and, after a few minutes of chaos, some retire discomfited to their seats while others rush excitedly to the president, and apparently record their transactions. The bell rings again, and the same scene recurs with another stock. After a time one of the recording angels reads the upshot of the various encounters with extraordinary rapidity, and the wheel of fortune, or the roulette, begins to spin again . . ."

As Solid as a Bank

The haughty towers of banks pervade the skies of San Francisco, and the wreckage of banks pervades its past. Since the days when merchants and express companies on Yerba Buena Cove began accepting gold dust in exchange for drafts on Eastern banks, this has been a banking town, for better or worse.

California's first constitution specifically forbade the chartering of banks that could issue notes that might be used as paper money. (Too much bad experience with that east of the Mississippi.) But "associations" of depositors flourished, guarding gold and silver, shipping bullion, and making loans at dazzling rates of interest (commonly 10 per cent a month). Unsupervised, undercapitalized, they grew (and popped) like balloons. In 1855 the local office of Page, Bacon & Co. of St. Louis shut its

Wells Fargo started as a mail carrier in 1852, got into banking by carrying gold. The modern bank that bears the name, after many mergers and acquisitions, is third largest in California, eleventh in the nation.

Amadeo Giannini's little Bank of Italy opened at Clay and Montgomery in 1904 (below). Now the giant Bank of America, it has world headquarters at California and Kearny Streets (right).

Failure of the Bank of California in 1875 set off a near-riot, plunged the Pacific Coast into economic depression (left). Failure of the San Francisco National Bank ninety years later, with most losses covered by insurance, was trivial by comparison (above). A saloon named "San Francisco National Bar" took over the office, sold drinks from tellers' windows under the slogan "Put your mouth where your money was."

doors, and in the ensuing panic half the banks in San Francisco collapsed, never to reopen.

Others have been more resilient. When the Bank of California failed in 1875, its brilliant organizer, William Ralston, went for a no-return swim, leaving $9.5 million in debts (equivalent to about $100 million today); but the bank itself, reorganized and refinanced, survives. Wells Fargo, a block up California Street, claims lineage to 1852; and Crocker National, the Proteus of the West Coast (variously Crocker-Woolworth, Crocker-First, Crocker-Anglo, and Crocker-Citizens), goes back to 1883. In this century, the financial climate of the Pacific has improved enough to nourish and sustain the world's biggest, most branching bank—the Bank of America.

Ladies with money, generally welcome at San Francisco banks, try out mohair sofas and octagonal writing tables in the Bank of Italy's Women's Department in 1925 (left). Overseen by an amiable guard, they line up with the men in a Wells Fargo branch decorated for the Christmas holidays in 1976.

Glittering Towers in Grapefruit Alley

The Golden Gateway project was San Francisco's major self-improvement effort of the 1960s—an ambitious, costly, politically difficult plan to move the wholesale produce district out of its crowded sheds at the edge of the downtown financial district and create there a new business and residential center.

That the plan succeeded is evidenced by these before-and-after photographs. That it was worth the trouble and expense remains a debatable question, at least among anti-progress folk, who argue, "Is San Francisco any better tall than it was short?"

Wholesalers who occupied lower Washington and Jackson Streets for more than a century liked to spread their wares on the sidewalk. Traffic was blocked from midnight to noon by trucks, forklifts, and lumpers. In 1868, when the district was already well established, the whole neighborhood turned out to pose with a 195½-pound melon (left). Below: Wilhelm Hahn's painting of Sansome Street between Commercial and Clay in the 1870s details teeming commerce down to the last stalk of celery.

Antiseptic pedestrian malls, paved with gleaming mosaic, run above street level, linking commercial and residential areas while traffic flows underneath. The Golden Gateway's blend of town houses, apartment towers, and major office buildings (below, right) is not exactly cozy but is less austere than many mid-century urban renewal projects.

A Square at the Center of Things

Back in the Beat Generation, a group of self-styled hipsters from upper Grant Avenue ran a tour bus one night to Union Square. No hassles. ("Don't bug the fuzz," they said.) They looked in the airline windows and checked out the absolutely unreal people lined up outside the St. Francis Hotel for the Nightclub Tour. ("Man, this is some kinda town. They even got a union for squares . . .")

No way, man. This block may *look* formal (at least from a distance), but square it has never been. It took its name from some noisy pro-Northern political exercises on the eve of the Civil War, and it has resounded with loudly voiced opinions ever since—opinions on Asian immigration, the Kaiser, the Nazis, capital punishment, abortion, lesbianism, the Vietnam War. In less polemical moods, Union Square has sheltered all the commercial and charitable manifestations one might expect on a 2.6-acre plot of more or less level open space at the center of the downtown shopping district: fund drives, blood drives, football rallies, rhododendron shows, weeks of amity with France and England, presidential visits, Christmas carols, Chinese New Years, and an annual bell-ringing contest for cable car conductors. (Now that *is* square!)

Robert I. Aitken's bouncy bronze figure of Victory, *girdled and trussed for an eighty-five-foot ascent to the top of the Dewey Monument's Corinthian column, is rarely viewed close up except by pigeons, which have kept her company for seventy-five years.*

Draped with flags and thronged with soldiers, Union Square radiates naïve and wholehearted imperialism in 1903 as President Theodore Roosevelt dedicates a monument to Commodore Dewey's coup at Manila Bay. ("You may fire when you are ready, Gridley.") In 1874 (below) a flagpole stood at the hub of the gravel pathways, and churches hemmed the square, giving it a deceitful look of propriety. Just east on Morton Street (now Maiden Lane) was the city's raunchiest red-light district.

The victory monument has acquired a new base and grown twelve feet to keep up with surrounding buildings. A medical-dental center at 450 Sutter has replaced the twin onion domes of Temple Emanu-el, and a Hyatt hotel (right) occupies the corner site of the many-chimneyed Pacific Union Club.

Mime Robert Shields perfected his artful mimicry of the gait and mannerisms of passers-by in Union Square. Dozens of imitators of the imitator now follow his craft, hoping to share Shields's success.

Streets and Shops of Fickle Fashion

The first merchants in San Francisco were Yankee traders, bringing mirrors, lace, and leather boots to barter for cattle hides and tallow.

With the gold rush came French shopkeepers—notably Félix Verdier, who sold a cargo of Parisian finery from the deck of a ship and thereby launched a family business that endured for 122 years. Verdier's City of Paris, like its chief competitor, the White House Department Store, succumbed at last to the changing habits of the tyrant public and the competition of new invaders: chain stores with famous names and national connections.

Like most downtown districts, San Francisco's retail center has been gnawed at recently by hungry rivals. Although the votaries of fashion have not entirely abandoned the familiar streets, they scatter their patronage now to shops in office towers in the Embarcadero Center, shops in Victorian flats on Union Street, shops in remodeled mustard works at Ghirardelli Square, and shops in vast suburban parking lots that once were prune orchards, marshes, or pastures.

At the lace department of the City of Paris in the early 1920s saleswomen wore black skirts and white blouses. At an Embarcadero Center boutique (below) they sometimes model the hats.

I. Magnin's has migrated a block up Geary Street since the picture at the upper right was taken on an afternoon shortly after World War I. The move (in 1948) upset the shopping habits of a few conservatives, but no one can deny that the tempo of activity is sprightlier at Stockton Street (above) than it used to be at Grant Avenue. In 1943 a window served as a sales office for United States "Victory Bonds" and (right) the store provided an air-raid shelter in the basement.

Shoppers waited in line to try out newly installed escalators at The Emporium on Market Street in 1936. Even during the Depression, it was easier to lure customers downtown than it is today.

"Mid all the din and grit of the city," wrote a visitor in 1902, "the brilliant array of bloom makes an oasis in the desert of stone." The oasis presumably was this one on Kearny Street, near the corner of Geary and Market, and the writer probably was driven to a frenzy of metaphor by the excitement of finding violets in December for only ten cents a bunch.

Bangles, Baubles, and Boutonnieres

For at least a century sidewalk vendors have been hawking fresh flowers on the street corners of San Francisco. The custom was formalized in the 1880s, when a throng of immigrant kids—Italians, Belgians, and Armenians, mostly—set up stands outside the San Francisco *Chronicle* at Kearny and Market Streets under the protection of the publisher, Mike de Young.

Since then, the flower stalls have spread and multiplied and blossomed into glass kiosks, canvas tents, and miniature cable cars. The sales principle remains the same: impulse buying, stimulated by an unexpected scent of lilac or the sudden proximity of a host of golden daffodils.

City officials, urged on by indoor florists, used to try from time to time to drive the flower sellers off the streets. Only a few years ago a member of the Board of Supervisors proposed tripling the license fee for sidewalk stalls. This time, however, the motive was not business rivalry. The supervisor had learned that some of the stands were grossing as much as $100,000 a year.

In 1937, when everyone was trying to decide whether we were just coming out of or just slipping back into a depression, a floral stand on Grant Avenue provided the consolation of spring blossoms and fresh daffodils (above). Vendors in the financial district now offer stained glass tulips (and real ones), translucent marigolds, ferns in Plexiglas, houseplants in hand-turned pottery, parking meter change, and weighty commentary on the Dow-Jones Averages.

Balloons at the BART station are one of the hazards of foot travel at Powell and Market. Others include soft pretzels, turquoise earrings, religious prophecy, accordion solos, and inflated plastic sharks.

Pit Stops and Brown Bags

In the cynical opinion of Montgomery Street, there is no such thing as a free lunch. There *used* to be, before it was wiped out by Prohibition, along with much else that was graceful and benign. Even now, one meets mature San Franciscans who are mesmerized by recollections of baked ham, hard-boiled eggs, cold poached salmon, and chafing dishes of navy beans, slowly simmered with salt pork and molasses, all served up as complimentary reinforcements with a ten-cent mug of beer.

No one has tried lately to bring back the free lunch (much less the dime beer), unless you allow credit for the meat balls in Happy Hour bars on Sansome Street or Belden. Nor has there been a crusade to revive the three-for-twos, which in the well-fed 1870s served three ten-cent dishes for two bits, to wit: a generous slice of roast beef with bread and butter and potatoes; a glass of wine, milk, coffee, tea, or chocolate; and a dish of pudding or a piece of pie.

What then of all our progress, our century of growth and gain? Take comfort in realizing that nowhere in Emperor Norton's San Francisco could you have found lox and cream cheese on a bagel, a pizza with double mushrooms, a taco, a souvlaki on folded pita, or a mashed avocado on seven-grain (hold the alfalfa sprouts).

And nary a sun-warmed bench to eat them on.

Not free but temptingly close to it, a cafe on Third Street bucked the Depression in 1932 by dropping prices to entice commuters walking from the Southern Pacific station. At a similar lunch counter nowadays, coffee and cake costs a dollar plus tax. Four eggs, any style, with toast, coffee, and a bowl of soup, could run more than $3.25. Below: Nickel coffee was still available—if rare—in 1953.

Bons vivants assemble for the noon spread at the Ideal Bar at California and Battery Streets in 1903. No napkins, but the management provided a couple of communal towels and a handy cuspidor.

Digging into the freebies in a familiar cartoon by Ed Jump is the grandiose free-loader of the 1870s, Emperor Joshua Norton I, accompanied by his courtiers, Bummer and Lazarus.

Picnicking on the sun-warmed terrazzo of Crown Zellerbach Plaza, a midday crowd enjoys the plashing of David Tolerton's flume-like bronze fountain and the backside exposure of brown-baggers perched like gulls along the Sansome Street wall. Nearby lunchrooms also run to Styrofoam cups and fresh air, have breezy names (Café de Wheels, Bar of America, Hamburger Mary's Organic Grill, the Personal Holding Company, the Suture Fancy Café).

Workers spread out lunch boxes and unwrap deli sandwiches in a sculptured garden at Embarcadero Center. As for noontime scrounging at the foot of Market Street, the pickings were better in the reign of Emperor Norton.

RTES

NATIONAL MARITIME MUSEUM AT SAN FRANCISCO

CHAPTER 2

Jason's Harbor

Viewed romantically, it is a mythic port of call: Jason's Harbor, the outpost of the argonauts, the matrix of an instant, gold rush city that astonished the world. In unromantic truth, the Port of San Francisco is a maritime sick bay, afflicted with obsolescence, redundancy, political interference, technological upheaval, economic irrationality, and provincial jealousies.

By broad definition, the "port" is, and always has been, the bay and its inland waters, reaching up to Crockett, Mare Island, Stockton, and Sacramento. By narrow jurisdiction, it is the waterfront of the city alone, a small (and proportionately shrinking) segment of the great ocean gate to northern California. It is this limited, urban waterfront, the anchor drop of the '49ers, that has enjoyed most of the glory, endured most of the strikes, and made most of the money for a century or more; and it is this waterfront that now is suffering most of the distress as cargo-handling business moves to wider shores.

Although the port of the past belonged exclusively to San Francisco, the port of the present is divided among a dozen rivalrous towns and harbor boards. If good sense prevails, the port of the future will belong to the entire Bay Area.

Broadway Wharf in the 1880s (left) accommodated a wooden-hulled down easter at left, two iron-hulled British three-masters, and a typical break-bulk cargo of crates and barrels. Today, many of the piers along the city's northern waterfront serve only as warehouses, restaurants, or fishing resorts for stylish sportsmen who cast their lines from car windows on stormy days.

Yerba Buena Cove, October 1848: Two small sailing craft and a rowboat are lightering supplies. (From a pencil sketch by C.A.M. Taber.)

The Embarcadero as many San Franciscans remember it—a busy but dignified boulevard of grayish-white warehouses stretching northward from Market Street on a rain-washed afternoon in 1938. In the late 1970s, the arched portal of Pier 1 may still be glimpsed across the parking lot, beyond the pillars of the double-decked vehicle freeway.

From an Anchor Drop to a World Port

During the quiet Mexican years, bumboats lightered bolts of cloth and kegs of nails into the shallow cove and dumped them on the beach. The outbound cargo waited in a rough corral, bellowing apprehensively. There were so many bones of slaughtered animals on the shore below Telegraph Hill that the whole town looked and smelled like an abattoir, which it was.

Gold rush merchants favored wooden wharves. They built one at the foot of every handy street, with scuttled ships and cheap-jack shops along the piers. As the land filled in between, the wharves became extensions of the streets, and the waterfront moved outward like a giant mud pie, oozing into the bay. Everyone, naturally, wanted a piece of the pie, and some got more than they deserved. In 1863 the state government intervened with the sublime object of ending municipal neglect, corruption in the sale of water lots, and piratical schemes to grab the whole harbor for various private owners.

For more than a century, the Port of San Francisco was an agency of the state. It was the state that issued millions in revenue bonds to build a great seawall of earth and riprap along the shore from the Presidio to the San Mateo County line; the state that built the finger piers; and the state that took the blame when, in the 1950s, the beautiful, legendary waterfront went out of style.

NATIONAL MARITIME MUSEUM AT SAN FRANCISCO

Yerba Buena Cove, late 1850: More than eight hundred vessels are at anchor in the gold rush harbor, many of them scuttled on mud flats that reach to Montgomery Street. This celebrated panorama, a two-part daguerreotype taken from the roof of a hotel on Portsmouth Square, is the earliest known photograph of San Francisco.

From a gull's view, the northern waterfront shows a century of change. In the 1877 Currier & Ives print (top) Market Street forms a diagonal (left of center) leading inland from a harbor jammed with square-riggers, side-wheel ferries, and barges. In the 1973 aerial photograph, the diagonal at left is Columbus Avenue. The seawall forming a smooth curve from Fisherman's Wharf to the Bay Bridge was built in the late 1870s–'80s, and most of the finger piers were built in the 1920s.

Laboriously unloading a coaler in the 1880s, a steam donkey powers a windlass dumping buckets of coal into a hopper that fills a procession of horse-drawn wagons.

Busy Days in Port

There still are a few men up and down the West Coast who remember when "mechanization" consisted of using a peavey to position a redwood log or a handhook to get hold of a 500-pound bale of jute. The beauty and terror of automation struck the Pacific ports only in 1942, when the first bulk shipment of Hawaiian sugar came into Crockett, on the upper San Francisco Bay. To unload 10,000 tons of sugar in sacks would have required 6,650 man-hours, plus a warehouse crew of eighty. In bulk, the cargo required only 1,000 man-hours and eight men in the warehouse.

In the late 1950s the International Longshoremen's and Warehousemen's Union and the Pacific Maritime Association, both having read the handwriting on the container, worked out an unprecedented agreement on mechanization and modernization that allowed shipowners to proceed with automation while guaranteeing workers compensatory wages and retirement.

Few persons outside the maritime industry understood that the agreement marked the end of San Francisco's established port facilities and their traditional "break-bulk" cargo handling.

Giant cranes on San Francisco's south waterfront lift huge prepacked vans directly from flatcars or trucks, cutting the turnaround time of ships, eliminating labor costs, pilferage, and damage.

NATIONAL MARITIME MUSEUM AT SAN FRANCISCO

Hand labor on the waterfront, 1906: a crew of Chinese draymen delivers a wagonload of neatly parceled food and bedding to a packing company's frieghter enroute to Alaska with Asians hired to clean and dress the salmon catch.

Hand labor on the waterfront, 1977: Longshoremen lift bags from a forklift onto a conveyor belt. Such traditional stevedoring is increasingly rare, even on the north waterfront, where slings, pallets, and lifts long ago replaced cargo hooks, hand hoists, and shovels. The main problem on the Embarcadero is not lack of machinery but lack of space for container storage, trucking and rail access. An added problem in 1978: Pacific Far East Line went into bankruptcy.

Longshoremen's president Harry Bridges was hero to management and labor when he negotiated automation agreements in the 1950s. In the '30s and '40s he had been America's most controversial labor leader, weathered jurisdictional disputes, marital troubles, and repeated government moves to deport him to his native Australia. Bridges retired in 1977 after forty-three years as head of ILWU.

NATIONAL MARITIME MUSEUM AT SAN FRANCISCO

The Embarcadero seawall from Telegraph Hill in the 1880s (above): Daring, imaginative, enormously expensive, this esplanade of concrete and stone took decades to build, added dozens of blocks to downtown San Francisco, allowed deep-water ships to come directly to shore. The seawall in the 1970s (right): Useless to container ships, supertankers, bulk carriers, and other modern vessels, the finger piers now accommodate a few mixed cargo ships and passenger liners. Many piers have been converted to office buildings, showrooms, or shops.

A Danish container ship, piled high with vans holding twenty tons each, steams past Alcatraz Island on her way to the Port of Oakland, where fenced cargo yards provide ample space for loading, unloading, and storing.

Where the Ships Are

It took almost a decade for the full impact of the technological revolution in cargo handling to strike San Francisco's northern waterfront. Then, suddenly, the old-fashioned piers along the seawall under Telegraph Hill were empty, and pitiful cries arose: "Where have the ships gone?"

The answer was that a few had gone up the bay to Stockton or Sacramento, some had gone to new bulk cargo terminals built by the Port of San Francisco south of the Bay Bridge, but most had wallowed gracelessly but efficiently into the Port of Oakland.

Many centrifugal forces tended to disperse the port: the construction of vehicle bridges, the growth of trucking, the scattering of industry into suburban and rural areas, the decline of manufacturing and warehousing in neighborhoods abutting the historic harbor. But containerization has been the strongest new influence to appear since the 1870s, when the seawall was built.

The first container ship to enter San Francisco Bay docked in Oakland in 1962. Seven years later, Oakland for the first time surpassed San Francisco in total tonnage, 5.3 million to 4.8 million tons. About 60 per cent of the Oakland tonnage was then in prepacked containers. By 1976 Oakland was handling 8.3 million tons a year, more than 80 per cent containerized, and was second only to New York in container tonnage in North America.

To know where the ships have gone, one need only watch them cross the bay. More difficult is to forecast the future of the wharves they have abandoned.

NATIONAL MARITIME MUSEUM AT SAN FRANCISCO

. . . and what became of the gold rush fleet

Beached in the shallows of Yerba Buena Cove, scores of Forty-niner vessels served time as shops, hotels, or warehouses, then were covered with fill and buried under the growing business district. A professional ship scuttler once estimated that a hundred brigs and barks were rotting beneath the streets of San Francisco: the brig Euphemia, *first city jail and "receptacle for the insane," deep in the mud at Battery and Sacramento Streets; the famous saloon (quondam storeship)* Apollo, *a few yards west; the storeship* Niantic *(pictured above), whose venerable timbers were unearthed by a contractor at Clay and Sansome Streets in 1978 and are now in the tender custody of the National Maritime Museum.*
In this map, black symbols mark known resting places of ships; white symbols show vessels that may have been removed to be dismantled; and shaded areas indicate: 1. Wells Fargo Bank; 2. Transamerica Corporation; 3. Federal Reserve Bank; 4. U. S. Customs House/Post Office; 5. Embarcadero Center; 6. Alcoa Building; 7. Golden Gateway Apartments; 8. Sidney G. Walton Square; 9. Hyatt Regency Hotel.

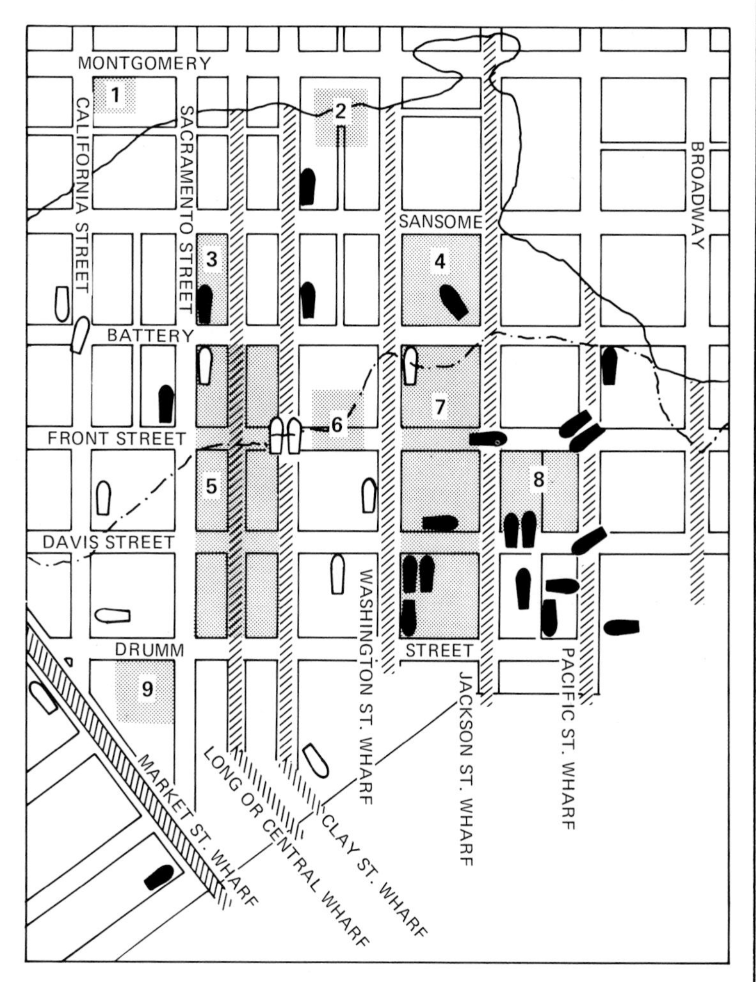

Down by the seawall in the 1880s landlubbers pose while a square-rigged cargo ship—probably one of hundreds that rounded the Horn each year in the great intercoastal trade—waits with all sails set. Below: a three-master again rests at dock in the 1970s, but now it is an exhibit in a museum of maritime history, and the setting is a park designed for sunbathing, strolling, and water sports.

A Window on the Bay

To city folk the port has always been more than just a place of employment, of sending and receiving, of arrival and departure. It has been a window on the bay and, by extension, on the world: a glimpse of blue horizons beyond the filing cabinets.

Now, as the city has grown away from commerce, and the cargo-handling business has moved southward and outward, emptying the piers along the seawall, new uses have come to the old waterfront that would have appalled the draymen, stevedores, and commission merchants of the nineteenth century: restaurants and souvenir shops, architects' drafting rooms and wax museums—and, right at the center of the Embarcadero, where longshoremen and strikebreakers fought with spiked clubs in the bloody '30s, a wide piazza in which office workers eat sandwiches, artisans peddle hand-dipped candles, and outraged citizens assemble to protest things.

The window opens today on a different bay, dancing with only memories of the port that was.

NATIONAL MARITIME MUSEUM AT SAN FRANCISCO

Pleasures of the port, 1906: A sun-warmed bollard for a seat, an apple seller for companionship, and the good sound of mallets, brushes, and cargo winches on a midwinter afternoon.

Pleasures (continued) 1976: Live bait, an Ike Walton rod, and a secret fishing pier; a guitar for solace in the lonely expanses of Embarcadero Plaza; and the latest from the Literary Guild under the gently roaring freeway.

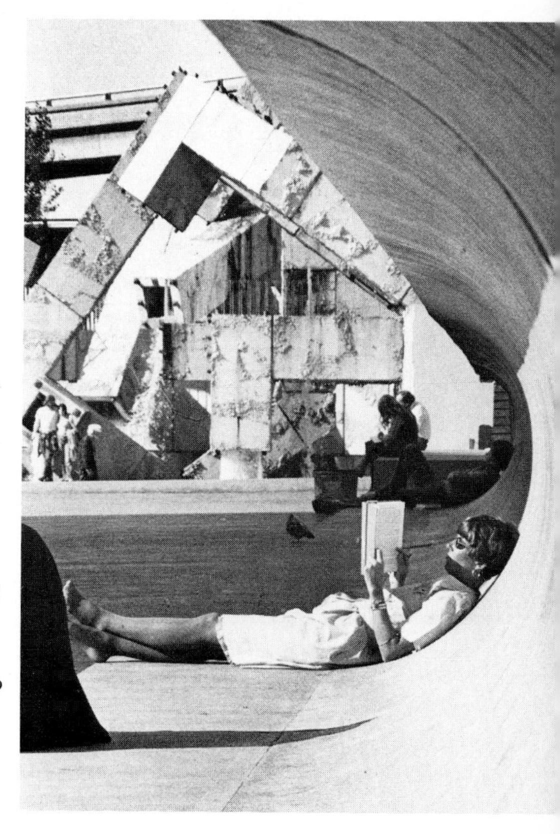

Fisherman's Wharf in the early years of this century had become a Sicilian monopoly. The men above, with sailors' instinct and a picture of the Madonna del Lume as their only compass, have brought a boatload of herrings through the foggy Golden Gate. Below: lateen-rigged feluccas line the Jones Street pier in 1901.

A Fine Kettle of Fish

Until recent years it would have been unnecessary to note that a slice of the waterfront of San Francisco between Taylor and Hyde Streets has been reserved for the past three quarters of a century as a harbor for the fishing fleet. Unnecessary, because the boats, the nets, the vats of steaming shellfish, and the fishermen manifested themselves so fragrantly, restlessly, and raucously that they became an unavoidable aspect of the city, and an endearing one.

The first custodians of this territory, which they occupied as a sort of ethnic mandate, were Italian emigrants from Genoa in the 1870s. But the Genovese had talents and interests that soon impelled them to fish in other waters—shopkeeping, winemaking, fruit canning, wholesaling, banking—and they sold their boats, one by one, to a later wave of settlers from Sicily. Most of the names around the Wharf these days—Alioto, Sabella, Castagnola (Paladini is a Genovese exception)—are those of Sicilians who took over around the turn of the century. In those days Fisherman's Wharf was a couple of finger piers where an incoming crew could unload a mixed catch, dry their nets, and cook a pot of *cioppino* on Friday night. It serves these functions still, but one has to look behind the souvenir shops to find them.

Fishing boats have changed with the city. They now carry radar, sonar, nylon nets, and they move by diesel power. The cost of technological progress is paid in the loss by industrial pollution of whole species of fish and crustaceans.

Baiting traditional woven traps, fishermen prepare for a trip out.

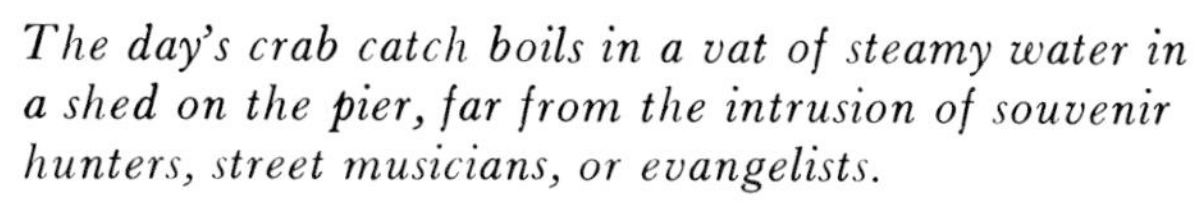

The day's crab catch boils in a vat of steamy water in a shed on the pier, far from the intrusion of souvenir hunters, street musicians, or evangelists.

NATIONAL MARITIME MUSEUM AT SAN FRANCISCO

Commerce at the wharf in 1935 (above) followed a crude formula: "Have crab, will sell." Contemporary shellfish merchandising requires costumed salesmen, Gulf shrimp, Alaska crab, chilled salads in take-away plastic dishes, souvenirs made in Taiwan.

The Dwarfing of the Wharf

Nowadays, we San Franciscans go to Fisherman's Wharf as strangers, appalled and embarrassed that a place of such simple, working origins—as simple as a man in a boat—should have acquired so many barnacles. The narrow ribbon of water is rimmed with blocks and blocks of freak museums, T-shirt shops, penny arcades, and quick-snack restaurants. Inland, like the sea foaming over the beach, are widening waves of motels, wine-tasting rooms, plant nurseries, art galleries, and automobile laundries.

The embarrassment is not that the restaurants and shops are bad; to the contrary, many of them are very good. The air around the wharf is lightly seasoned with garlic dressing and the iodine of crab shells, and the people drifting arm in arm through the arcades appreciate the postcards and seashells and pottery cable cars.

The embarrassment is that we have created an amusement park so popular, so irrelevant to its founding institution. The fishing fleet could be scat-

Allure of the wharf on a sunny afternoon centers on shoulder-to-shoulder waterfront restaurants, many named for families who started here as fishermen. The array of sideshows, some owned by the same families, includes museums and helicopter rides.

tered, the processing sheds closed, and the harbor filled with rubble, all without disrupting the brisk tempo of getting and spending onshore.

In the long run this might be advisable. Fishing has been in decline, and the present extent of the harbor is a disappointment to people who have paid to park and have wandered long through shooting galleries and wax museums, searching for the central shrine. Relocated at, say, Hunters Point, the fishing fleet again would be impressive and unexpected.

Much of the current progress at Fisherman's Wharf has been inspired by the same port management that has been struggling with the problem of adapting nineteenth-century piers to modern cargo handling. The licensing of tourist traps on port property is one answer to what to do with the waterfront, although it is not the answer we would have given. There is only one Fisherman's Wharf; we have no other; and the one we cared for is irremediably spoiled.

A Gateway on the Bay

As San Marco's was to Venice, the Ferry Building and its plaza were to San Francisco—a doorstep on the water during the city's years of marriage to the sea. Thousands of travelers, coming by train from the East, disembarked from the Oakland ferry into these thundering gray corridors. Millions of commuters scurried up the ramps and down the brass-edged stairs, rushing toward the clang of Market Street, the brine, the breeze, the salty mist. San Franciscans boasted that the Ferry Building was the busiest terminal in America, second in the world to London's Charing Cross.

The first Ferry Building (1877–96), with its squat wooden clock tower, cobbled turnabout, and billboards advertising land auctions in South Berkeley, was only an ugly carbarn on a quay. A few unsentimental critics say the present tower is not much better. Built of gray Colusa sandstone, and opened in 1898, it is a reproduction of the belltower (quondam Moorish minaret) adjoining the Cathedral of Seville.

Yet, in its years of useful popularity, the 235-foot spire became a symbol of the city. Even now, converted into an office building, half hidden by a brutally designed freeway, it remains an emblem, a mute reproach, giving daily evidence of disrespect for tradition and loss of direction in a city that professes to have a delicate reverence for the living past.

Isolated from the city by a double-deck freeway and the parking lots beneath it, the clock tower pokes up numbly, like a thumb anesthetized for amputation. A glimpse of the tower, dwarfed by new buildings, at the foot of narrow Commercial Street (right) is a poignant reminder to older San Franciscans of days when the Ferry Building epitomized the city's graceful tempo.

First ferry landing place (1877) was a combination pier and carbarn with a row of sheds on the landward side labeled with enticing destinations of the Central Pacific Railroad: Cloverdale, Portland, Red Bluff, New York . . . Right: Newsboys offer the Evening Bulletin, *the* Post, *and other now defunct papers to commuters striding toward the boats on an evening before World War I.*

Above: The Tamalpais, *built in 1857, and the side-wheeler* Alameda I, *vintage of 1866, pass with a friendly beep one morning in the early 1890s. Although such veterans as these were retired before the turn of the century, the style and rhythm of ferry service changed little during its hundred-year reign. Right: Sleekest, speediest of Golden Gate Transit's new ferries, the* San Francisco *(on a test run), is 165 feet long, weighs less than 100 tons, and carries 750 passengers. The largest commute ferries in the '30s averaged more than 290 feet in length, weighed up to 2,700 tons, and carried 4,000 passengers.*

Fading Trails of Foam

Our century of ferryboats began in 1850 with a tiny steamer called the *Kangaroo* that made two runs a week between a boggy spot that now is Oakland and the shallow cove that became downtown San Francisco. The transbay fare was stiff: passengers—$1.00; horses and wagons—$3.00 each; cattle—$3.00 a head; hogs—$1.00; freight—four bits a hundredweight. Once launched, however, the ferries would endure and flourish, streaking the bay with a web of froth from Alameda on the south, to Vallejo on the north. In the 1930s, Southern Pacific had forty-three vessels and the Key System a dozen, and the two competing companies carried 40 million passenger trips a year.

One by one, automobile bridges leaped the straits and narrows. Electric trains took over the transbay commute in 1940. Less than twenty years later, the last passenger boat crossed from Oakland, bringing a trainload of transcontinental travelers into the city. A bus replaced it, so to speak, although no bus could take the place of a magnificent white goddess, honking round the southern cliffs of Yerba Buena Island, halfway across the bay.

Crumbling on shore, the vessels have become museums, showboats, scraps of iron. Their descendants are a token fleet of swifter, smaller boats that run only to Marin county, north of the Golden Gate. They are paid for, grudgingly, by drivers on the overcrowded Golden Gate Bridge.

Below: Southern Pacific ferries head for Oakland on a fall afternoon in 1939, passing exposition buildings to the left on Treasure Island.
Right: Smaller ferries, almost four decades later, dock at a modest pier north of the Ferry Building.

A Commute by Water

A man from Berkeley finished *War and Peace* aboard the *Sacramento.* A woman from Fruitvale knitted a sweater a year for each of her twelve grandchildren. Thousands of other commuters played endless tournaments of pedro, threw crusts of Remar bread to the strident gulls (whose mid-air fielding was the envy of the Oakland Acorns and the San Francisco Seals), walked the decks to Singapore and back, grappled for cameras and watchbands among the mounds of candy-coated peanuts in the nickel slot machines, or ate, with wolfish speed, the apple pie, the butterhorns, and the Key Route corned beef hash. Once in a while, some passenger who had been standing alone by the rail, absorbed in thought, would vanish into the fog.

Nowadays, you can see the old *Eureka,* painted and polished, at the Maritime Museum—a relic like the *Vasa* or the *Cutty Sark.* Or you may take the Sausalito boat, play dominoes, eat a Danish pastry, and feed the raisins to a gull. Some people say it is a lot the same.

Twin-stacked Alameda, *bringing a cargo of tired daddies home to the East Bay on an afternoon in the early 1940s, was one of Southern Pacific's largest passenger boats (292 feet long, 1,879 seats). Well-bred passengers wore hats and vests and put their faith in U. S. Steel and* The Saturday Evening Post.

Commuter traffic on today's Golden Gate is a trickle to yesterday's torrent, but those who loved the ferries see it as the portent of a future of daily boat rides.

A boon to boat commuters, past and present, is leisure for breakfast, snacks, cocktails. Right, two flappers circa 1928 order up ham sandwiches and milk shakes at fifteen cents each. Southern Pacific ferries served three thousand muffins, doughnuts, and Danish pastries every day. On the Sausalito run in the 1970s (above) coffee and doughnuts are still in demand.

The frosty young women at left, dressed in the fashionable pleats and scarves of the mid-'20s, presumably are en route to the city after the morning rush for a little shopping at The White House, a matinee at the Tivoli, and tea-dancing at the Pavo Real. Below: On the Marin ferry in the '70s ten-speed bikes travel with the commuters, and the only favored headwear is a watch cap.

GREEN

CHAPTER 3

At Home on the Hills

"How many hills are there in San Francisco?" asked a sightseer on the morning tour.

"Seven, lady," the guide answered, as wrong as he was self-assured. The passengers, observing that the total was amazingly like that of Rome, nodded and murmured, counting hills on their fingers, happily unaware that no one agrees on the number of hills in San Francisco, much less on what to call certain of the smaller ones. Some years ago, the San Francisco *Chronicle,* in a series of articles on local protuberances, counted up to forty-two, including two that had more or less disappeared (Rincon and Irish) and leaving out Cathedral, which had not yet been named. The number probably is as accurate as any other.

By any standard, San Francisco is a lumpy town. Rivalrous Oaklanders across the bay see this as confirming evidence that the location of the city was a historic mistake, but most San Franciscans regard their corrugated landscape as a precious gift. The hills are a constant, mild stimulus, lifting one's spirit and expanding one's horizon. To drive, to ride, to walk them is unnerving, surprising, exhilarating.

The hills create another tension, which is social. They open and close visions of the future. Living on a hill is an achievement, a sort of geographic privilege. Down in the narrow alleys of the Mission District, out in the rolling Sunset, San Franciscans dream of clinging like bighorn sheep to the ultimate slope of Vallejo Street, the piney crags of Edgehill.

The poet George Sterling, who usually lived on one or another of the hills, wrote a frequently quoted ode that concludes, "At the end of our streets—the stars." In the flatlands it has been observed that stars are not equally visible from every street.

Below: The crest of Montgomery Street on Telegraph Hill was a rural playfield for children in long-sleeved dresses in the early 1920s. Today the street is paved and is dotted with trees, and concrete stairs descend the bluff, but the same round-cornered houses still oversee the changing city.

Sprinkled with shanties, the naked summit offered a mediocre vista of Yerba Buena Island and the East Bay in 1931, just before construction of the Bay Bridge. The small houses at center right are on what was First Street.

A Vanished Eminence

Rincon Hill was San Francisco's first neighborhood of fashion, and its downfall was so sudden, its ruin so complete, as to suggest that neighborhoods, like kings, are subject to the tragic force of hubris.

Rincon was the southern horn on the crescent of Yerba Buena Cove, the city's primitive shoreline on the bay. Nothing particularly recommended it as a place of residence except its tempered climate and its respectable distance from the dives and whorehuts at the north end of the cove. Still, someone made the move. (Records name John Gihon, one of three collaborators in the first of hundreds of histories of San Francisco.) By 1860, Rincon was *the* place to live, especially if you were, or were married to, a banker, a military officer, or a Southern gentleman. All the best (or richest) people thronged within the bounds of Second, Folsom, Spear, and Brannan Streets. Senator Gwin gave eggnog parties; Mrs. Hall McAllister served oyster suppers; Mrs. Peter Donahue drove out in a glass-walled carriage. An English promoter laid out an oval garden on the western slope, in the style of the private parks of London, and gave keys to homeowners around the rim of his "South Park."

Yet, in 1879, when Robert Louis Stevenson climbed the hill to meet a fellow-writer, Charles Warren Stoddard, he found "a new slum, a place

Leveled to form a base for the bridge, Rincon Hill is now a tidy flatland of warehouses and parking lots, seen here from an office building perched on the last remnant of the hill—a knob of red rock under the freeway ramps.

Unkindest cut of all lowered Second Street in 1869 so trucks could rumble through. In a decade the prosperous neighborhood became a slum.

of precarious, sandy cliffs, deep, sandy cuttings, solitary, ancient houses, and the butt ends of streets."

Through the political manipulations of a real estate exploiter named John Middleton, the hundred-foot hill had been sliced open like a melon to create a highway to the south waterfront. The gentry had fled. The hill was left to artists, goats, and stubborn old millionaires who refused to cut their losses and get out. When in the 1930s the state proposed to anchor the western footing of the Bay Bridge upon this ravaged rock, hardly anyone knew where Rincon Hill was—an erstwhile Valhalla, gone without a trace.

Anna Downey Donahue and her sister Eleanor Martin lived at Second and Bryant Streets (far left), now the site of a large printing plant and larger bridge approach. Typical of Rincon's tranquil ambiance was the Classical Revival home at right, photographed in the 1870s by C. E. Watkins, and, like the hill, long gone.

A Mighty Pile of Gold and Silver

For the sake of harmony, we shall refrain from debating here the origin of the name "Nob Hill." Whether it be a corruption of snob or nabob, or a misspelling of knob, is less important than that it replaced the inappropriate and mushy-mouthed "Fern Hill" in the 1870s, just when the profits of the transcontinental railroad, interocean shipping, and Comstock silver mines began to show up in the form of elaborate domestic architecture along California Street between Powell and Hyde.

As Rincon Hill faded, Nob Hill flowered, favored by the installation of Mr. Hallidie's marvelous cable cars in 1873. Within a decade, the Big Four, owners of the Central Pacific, the Silver Kings of Nevada, the exploiters of grain and cattle, sugar and spice, sealskins and lamp oil, all had moved as if on cue to the crown of the city.

The mansions are gone now, devoured by the fires of 1906, but Nob Hill has held its high tone for more than a century. Many of the city's most expensive hotels and restaurants, capitalistic clubs, and fancy apartment houses now occupy the ridge where Jane Stanford poured tea, Charley Crocker poured champagne, and Jimmy Flood poured almost anything that would fit in a glass.

Castles of the Robber Barons in the 1880s (right to left along California Street) were James Flood's $1.5 million Connecticut brownstone; David Colton's Italianate palazzo, later owned by Collis P. Huntington; and Charles Crocker's Gothic fortress. Only the Flood mansion (now the Pacific Union Club) remains. Huntington Park and Grace Cathedral occupy the other lots; and Mark Hopkins's huge house (from which the upper photo was taken) became the site of the Mark Hopkins Hotel (from which the lower photo was taken).

Well groomed, well fed, and well behaved, Nob Hill's permanent residents are a small aristocracy who sun themselves and walk their terriers, ignoring the rush of taxis and transients. While preschool children dabble in the Tortoise Fountain (gift of a descendant of the Crocker family), scholars troop off to class at the Cathedral School for Boys.

Russian Hill: Island of the Blest

Once it was a rocky goat pasture, named for a patch of sacred earth where the crewmen of a Russian sealer buried their dead on a fur-hunting expedition in the 1820s. Later, it was a bohemia of sorts, inhabited by writers who had done all right with poems and novels about Romantic California. Today it is one of the last hilltops in San Francisco with both social cachet and (a few) single-family homes.

Through it all, Russian Hill has been a darling of fortune. Out of the few dozen wood-frame structures that escaped destruction in the 490-block area of the earthquake-fire of 1906, most were on this hilltop, on a short stretch of Vallejo Street. A stubborn band of residents, ignoring orders to evacuate, fought off flames for two hellish days, scooping up pots of water from old cisterns, beating out falling embers with wet mops. The pictures above show how the survivors looked in 1906, floating in a sea of rubble, and how they looked in 1977, surrounded by encroaching towers.

"House of the Flag," at 1656 Taylor Street, won renown in 1906 when tenants defiantly flew Old Glory as flames climbed the hill, thereby inspiring Army fire fighters to come to the rescue with wet sand and bottled seltzer water. Left and below: the house in '06, encircled by ruins. Right: the house stands vacant, patched with plywood, after surviving another fire, in 1975, its future as uncertain as the quality of its roof.

The Hill Hauled Round the World

In every city there are neighborhoods where the act of taking up residence constitutes admission to an elite. Russian Hill once had that quality, before apartment houses crashed the club; Potrero Hill has struggled to attain it; and a few sequestered streets—Edgewood, Hill, Edgehill, and Fifth Avenue north of Lake Street—have developed this particularity. None has more of a sense of conspiratorial intimacy than Telegraph Hill, San Francisco's Greenwich Village, its Beacon Hill, its Sixth Arrondissement. Smirking, the favored fraternity puffs up and down the narrow stairways, coming and going among buffet suppers and Sunday brunches, pausing now and then to turn out songs and poems, books and paintings in celebration of this little paradise, which has not always been held in such esteem.

The Mexicans ignored it; the first Yankees used the crest as a signal post and the slope as a gun

A marine observation tower with semaphore arms to signal the approach of ships gave Telegraph Hill its name in 1850. The rustic landscape at left, probably painted by a passenger on one of the anchored ships, shows on the southeast slope the primitive artillery post for which Battery Street (now many yards lower) was named.

Looking from the hill toward the Golden Gate in the 1860s (left), photographer Eadweard Muybridge shared the view with Mrs. O'Reilly's cows. Human beings now monopolize the parking space and the coin-operated binoculars. No one has met a cow here in years.

mount; and gold rush squatters built shacks as far up as one could crawl. Skippers returning in ballast to Europe or the States blasted chunks off the sides to fill the holds of their ships, and the red Californian rock wound up in the pavements of New York and Liverpool. Quarry operators gnawed relentlessly at the eastern slopes. Only the poor could endure such living conditions. Around the turn of the century the Irish, in Wallace Irwin's words, lived at the top av it, the Dagos at the base av it, "and every tin can in the knowledge of man is scatthered all over the face av it."

Telegraph Hill Observatory, a restaurant-bar-concert hall of Teutonic ancestry, lorded over the east slope from 1882 to 1903, losing money for a series of owners despite such promotional efforts as a five-cent cable car up Greenwich Street and bloody combat between a Scottish cavalry swordsman and various armored challengers.

The Private Life of a Public Peak

The top of Telegraph Hill always has been grabbed off, one way or another, by Outsiders: first a semaphore, then a cow pasture, next a goat farm, and, for the last hundred years, a public park. Trickling in from the top down, artists and writers invaded the Irish highlands in the 1920s. By the same insidious route, advertising agents, psychiatrists, and stockbrokers have been oozing in ever since, bringing along their European sports cars, imported gin, three-piece suits, and other detestable evidences of ability to pay high rent for a neat view.

The one-room bargain shanties and garden cottages are disappearing. Luxury studios and condominiums are proliferating, bemoaned by every resident who arrived here the day before. "The Hill is losing its character," they say—and it is true. That any locality could have lost character so rapidly for so many years and still have retained so much of it is one of the pleasant miracles of our beloved city.

Nozzle-like Coit Tower, built in 1934 with a bequest from the city's richest fire buff, Lillie Hitchcock Coit, weighs on the hill like a crown on its king. Inside are murals by local artists under the influence of Diego Rivera; at the base, a ruff of eucalyptus trees and a crowded parking pad. To residents of the hill, the tower is a minor irritation in a breezy purlieu of cats, geraniums, French bread, mama-papa stores, caffè espresso bars, apartment hunters, parking problems, and incomparable vistas.

Climbing the Top Ridge

Twin Peaks, for obvious reasons, was known to the Spaniards as "The Maiden's Breasts." The hummocks to the south, for obscure reasons, are called Diamond Heights. Together, they form the central massif of the San Francisco Peninsula and the last undeveloped highlands to defy even the cable car.

For the motorcar, however—ah-ha! The formidable Twin Peaks Climb became an annual show of power. And when the internal combustion engine is heard, can the tract developer be far behind?

During the 1930s and '40s, buildings climbed the peaks in "terraces," a San Francisco euphemism for row houses built on the contour lines of steep grades. In the '50s they came in larger clusters called "manors." By the '60s the Redevelopment Agency had bought up Diamond Heights, redrawn the unbuildable gridiron streets, and introduced to the crown of the city "planned unit development." The heights, as a result of these attentions, are swathed in pastel stucco. Only the brown *pechos* remain unclothed, more or less as the Spaniards saw them.

Nervy drivers challenging the figure-eight around the lonely Twin Peaks in the 1920s (top) drew curious spectators, most of whom figured that it was a nice place to visit but you wouldn't want to live there. Sightseers and tour buses still follow the same curves to the lookout at Christmas Tree Point, but houses have climbed almost to the edge of the Grande Corniche.

Jersey cows on Good Brothers' Twin Peaks Ranch were bemused by a rare snowfall in December 1932 (above). The white ribbon at center right is a reservoir; the black line at left, O'Shaughnessy Drive, under construction. The view today (right) is cowless and cottages ring the pasture. Still, the area retains a rural look unusual in San Francisco. The wooded hill at right is Mount Davidson (938 feet), highest in the city.

Diamond Heights from Twin Peaks Boulevard and Duncan Street (bottom left) in 1963 was innocent of human habitation, although the Redevelopment Agency had laid out sweeping boulevards. In fifteen years it has become a lively neighborhood with views that box the compass and winds that shiver the timbers.

Filling in the Dunes

When they came to the Outside Lands—the lands that lay beyond the historic limits of the Mexican pueblo of Yerba Buena—the city fathers decreed a gridiron plan of alphabetic streets and numbered avenues, stretching over humps and hollows out to the margin of the sea.

First, they annexed an area they called, logically but unromantically, the Western Addition. Beyond it was an open district known, even less enticingly, as the Great Sand Waste. Out in the G.S.W. squatters built cottages and barns among the dunes, drew brackish water from the ground with windmills, exacted tolls from carriages enroute to the Cliff House, and shared the summer fog with sand fleas, gulls, and foxes.

Acre by acre, the city devoured the dunes, and the dunes became the Richmond District (north of the park) and the Sunset District (south of it). The sand resisted, blowing back in stinging clouds against the outer walls. It was not until the 1930s that the ubiquitous row houses poured across the billowing desert west of Twin Peaks, creating almost overnight a new San Francisco of small white villas with tunnel entrances and venetian blinds—a visible symbol of middle-class conformity, an easy target for snobbish disparagement. In a decade the timeless sands were gone, leaving only a few vacant lots with tufts of sedge and pads of ice plant and a swirl of grit along the alphabetic streets on blustery afternoons.

West of Golden Gate Heights few streets penetrated the wasteland in 1928. The same view fifty years later (right) shows cheek-to-cheek houses marching south in solid ranks from Golden Gate Park, at center right, toward the county line.

Plowing, planting, and mulching with tons of street sweepings, city workers tamed the western edge of Golden Gate Park, a Saharan waste in 1871. Thousands of row houses accomplished the same task in residential areas without aid of trees or grass, alas.

Eleventh Avenue south of Noriega Street in 1926 (top right) was a line of utility poles and a wooden footpath through dunes. A year later (center) it had been graded into an uninviting country lane. The same block today (lower right) is virtually indistinguishable from hundreds of others west of Twin Peaks. The shingled cottage with its sheltering cypress trees has disappeared, but the utility poles endure, capped with an extra tier of wood and wire.

Variations on a theme by contractor—above: The white cliffs of Daly City, a suburb ruthlessly conquered by invading San Francisco row houses (give 'em an inch, they'll take a mile). Assorted fronts and identical backs create a pattern of pastel stripes across the hills. If you stare at the bottom row for a few seconds, the houses suddenly swivel ninety degrees from left to right. Below left: A shingled row in Diamond Heights was designed in the 1970s to create a rhythmic pattern, whereas the modest, 1930 cottages in the outer Sunset District (right) are as different as peas in a pod.

Row, Row, Row Your House

In recent years it has been customary to blame the popularity of the San Francisco row house (also known as the ticky-tacky box) on (a) the prevailing westerly winds; (b) a succession of shortsighted city governments; (c) Henry Doelger, a Dutch-born building contractor who discovered in the 1930s that many families would rather live on their own thirty-seven-foot-wide patch of sand with their own four-by-six lawn than in an apartment surrounded by virgin forest; (d) the Gellert brothers, who perfected a technique of squeezing out toothpaste-like strands of "Sunstream Houses" in diverse styles and colors with identical floor plans; or (e) the depraved taste and financial desperation of several generations of home buyers.

All these factors and malefactors contributed to the takeover of southwestern San Francisco and northern San Mateo County by endless ranks of look-alikes. But long before Doelger and Gellert arrived on the sand hills, San Francisco had been garlanded with strings of narrow wooden boxes attributed (without authorization) to the influence of Sir Charles Eastlake, the English art critic. Most of these close-order cottages (which are much admired nowadays by people who detest Daly City row houses) date from the 1880s, when a designer named John C. Pelton, Jr., published a book beguilingly titled *Cheap Dwellings*.

What home builder could resist? Pelton's Eastlake cottages took on bay windows and became San Francisco row houses. Their descendants are with us, under construction to this day.

Aristocratic "Oriel Row," built in 1889, was the fullest flowering of the Queen Anne-Eastlake style in San Francisco row houses. Designed by an architect from St. Louis named Absalom J. Barnett for a block-long site on the north side of elegant Eddy Street in the Western Addition, these mansions had acquired fire escapes and date palms and had lost class when this photograph was taken in the early 1930s.

Streetcar scrimmage on lower Market Street frustrates commuters headed for East Bay ferries on a damp October afternoon in 1937. The trolley turning right-oblique (at left center) is moving to an outside track to pick up and discharge passengers on a loop at the Ferry Building. Today the same intersection (right) is deceptively placid. BART trains and Muni streetcars move under the street; the surface is left to cars, buses, and California Street cable cars, which still terminate across the way at Market and Drumm. Opposite page: A stalled bus clogs traffic on a Friday evening in March 1975. Nothing new.

CHAPTER 4

Getting Around in a City of Hills and Water

Transportation, which is second only to taxation as the world's most tiresome subject, has always been a municipal obsession in San Francisco. The reason is everywhere apparent. Hills and gullies, gulfs and inlets parcel out the territory, and the whole scene is 3,000 miles from what used to be called "The States" in the days when it took six months to get there.

From the beginning, enterprising folk made commercial assaults upon this inconvenient terrain: footbridges across the swamp that now is Jackson Street; bumboats to the tidal plain later known as Oakland; steamers up the bay to Petaluma, Benicia, and Sacramento City; pony postage to the distant East; a neatly planked toll road that charged four bits to trot one's horse and rig out to Mission Dolores for the bull-and-bear fights and a milk punch at Charley Brown's.

But nothing goes out of fashion faster than modes of transportation, and San Francisco, having no wish to be quaint (no matter what you may have heard or read), has never stopped rebuilding, revising, and throwing away its transit system.

The first civic passion (unsatisfied until the transcontinental railroad was completed in 1869) was to achieve a swifter passage to the East. Then it was links across the bay—and that has entailed, over the years, fleets of ferries, buses, and trains, bridges, trestles, helicopters, and an underwater tube. Meanwhile, progressive citizens hankered to get rid of all the marshes (by filling) and all the hills (by dumping them into the marshes) and to improve all the peaks that could be neither leveled nor ignored, by running cable railroads up the sides.

It made for an exciting go-round. After a cable ride in 1889, Rudyard Kipling reported: "They turn corners almost at right angles, and, for all I know, may run up the sides of houses." A woman from Connecticut was so panic-stricken on the Hyde Street line that she had to be wrapped in a blanket and lifted off in mid-block. And the advent of motor cars grinding up and down the hills struck witnesses as the climax of fearsome technology. A British journalist, visiting in 1922, said that he rode around in a "continual state of terror, as automobiles hurl themselves down streets which in England we would call precipices."

"Bad motorists," he concluded, "go to San Francisco when they die."

The last horsecar made its final run up Market Street to Sutter Street in 1913, loaded with cops and politicians.

Dobbin's Day

For fifty fragrant, flyblown years, horses dominated the city, pulling carriages, trolleys, trucks, and fire engines along the cobbled streets. Flat-bottomed barges brought hundreds of thousands of tons of hay down the Sacramento River every year to fuel the urban transportation system. Street sweepers collected ten thousand tons of refuse and carted it out to Golden Gate Park to fertilize the sandy wastes. Air pollution was merely an aesthetic consideration. Neither smog nor the word to describe it had been invented.

Step by step, miraculous machines assumed the burdens of the horse: in the 1870s the cable car; in the '90s the electric trolley; and, soon after World War I, the motorcar. With the burdens went the beast who bore them. For fifty odorless, flyless years now, the horse has been a curiosity in San Francisco, a creature ridden by policemen in the park and by cowboy actors in parades, and blue-white fumes hang in the air where pungent droppings once smoldered in the fog.

Mayor James Rolph gives a testimonial dinner to two old whites before their last run. Horses wore carpet overshoes to prevent their slipping on asphalted streets.

Unique "Balloon Car," designed by Henry Casebolt, rotated on a four-wheel truck. At the end of the line the driver released a pin, drove the team in a half-circle, and went back the way he came. This car ran out Mission Street to Woodward's Gardens in the early 1870s.

Lone horsecar in the trolley merry-go-round at the foot of Market Street in 1910 was owned by a tenacious franchise holder who had a profitable run from the Ferry Building to Sutter and Sansome Streets.

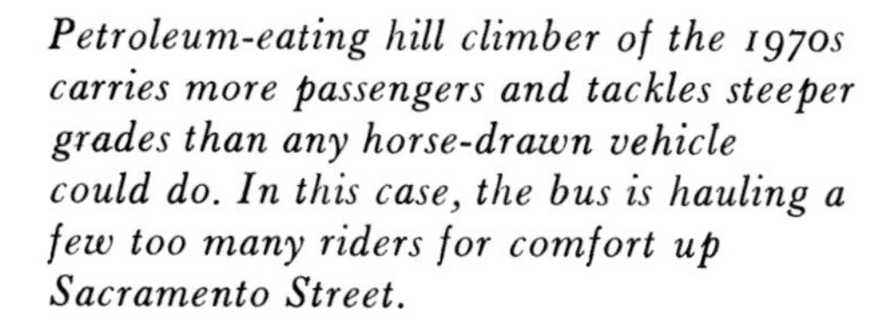

Petroleum-eating hill climber of the 1970s carries more passengers and tackles steeper grades than any horse-drawn vehicle could do. In this case, the bus is hauling a few too many riders for comfort up Sacramento Street.

The Cable that Conquered the Hills

The chivalric rescue of a lady trapped in a cable car slot titillated readers of the Police Gazette *in 1881. Caption: "She put her little foot in it."*

Andrew S. Hallidie, who developed a patented hand grip with which a passenger car could be clamped to a cable and thereby whisk uphill like a skier on a rope tow, was a manufacturer of wire ropes, a circumstance that has led some commentators to conclude that Hallidie was motivated by a desire for gain.

Whatever his motives, Hallidie became a civic hero in San Francisco, where his Clay Street line, opened in 1873, permitted grateful millionaires to perch their castles on the crest of Nob Hill and afforded even common folk a thrilling ride across the peaks. By 1880 the line had been extended to Van Ness Avenue and was carrying two million passengers a year at five cents a ride. Before long, San Francisco had eight cable car companies operating six hundred cars, and cables had replaced horse-drawn trolleys even in the flatlands. A half-dozen other cities (New York, Chicago, Philadelphia, and Kansas City among them) had adopted cable cars. And Mr. Hallidie—well, he *did* gain.

Although time has rung many changes on California Street since the 1870s (left), there are comforting signs of immortality in the hill, the tower of Old St. Mary's, and the double-ender car approaching Grant Avenue.

Andrew Hallidie's Clay Street car skated up the grade from Portsmouth Square for the first time at 5 A.M. on a foggy day in August 1873. By that act of self-levitation without visible means of propulsion, the cable car at once endeared itself to the capitalists of San Francisco, who crowded aboard in top hats and silk bonnets and immediately began buying hilltop real estate.

SALON
OLD SAN FRANCISC
Sts.
MJB

The Enduring Charms of the Dinkies

In most cities cable cars lasted as a form of public transit for only a decade or two. In San Francisco, for good enough reasons (geography, tourism, sentiment), they have hung on for more than a century, establishing an ineradicable position as the totem of the modern city. Cable cars crop up in songs and verses, books and movies, medals and certificates, and in thousands upon thousands of ashtrays, lamp stands, tie clasps, greeting cards, T-shirts, planters, salt-and-pepper shakers. . . .

When the cable cars achieved their centennial year, commemorated by a new tidal wave of souvenirs, the city government, which from time to time has attempted to scrap the whole system, signaled its capitulation by building a BRAND NEW, authentically ancient cable car. Cost: $40,000.

Above: Lined up at turntable near the Ferry Building, dozens of United Railroad cable cars trundle along Market Street in 1905. The modern cable car turntable (at right and opposite page) is almost identical to those of the nineteenth century. On summer weekends would-be riders wait in block-long queues to crowd aboard. To patrons on the Sutter Street line in 1905 (below) open cars were commonplace. At that time the city had more than a hundred miles of cable slots.

TIONAL MARITIME MUSEUM AT
N FRANCISCO

Age and rarity have brought veneration to this primitive dinkie from the city's first cable line. Dusted and polished, it commands a ten-foot track in a cable car museum. Dozens like it wound up in steel pots.

End of the Line

Scattered like discarded toys, obsolete streetcars lay among the dunes along the ocean beach a few miles south of Mayor Adolph Sutro's mansion at Land's End in the 1890s. It was a time of economic depression. Jobs and homes were scarce. With Sutro's backing, colonists invaded the graveyard of trolleys, put up lace curtains, raised picket fences, planted geraniums. For three decades, Carville sheltered a relaxed little community of full-time passengers.

After the 1906 earthquake and fire, street railways offered antiquated cars at twenty-five dollars each (bell included), delivered to your lot. Hundreds were set up in what is now the Sunset District, along unpaved lanes named Elegy, Elysian, and Piccadilly Streets.

Few streetcars nowadays would pass the building code. Crushed into scrap, old cars disappear. A half-dozen trolley houses, well camouflaged, hide among the stuccoed villas of the outer Sunset. Only cable cars live forever, rumbling on rubber tires around convention halls, loaded with dentists up from Fresno wearing buttons that say, "Hi! I'm Al."

Shingled streetcars with draperies and indoor plumbing housed refugees from the 1906 disaster. These mobile homes occupied a wedge-shaped block between California and Cornwall Streets at Sixth Avenue.

Transit car dump near the southwest corner of Golden Gate Park supplied prefab homes for Carville. Below: A trolley cottage, still standing at 1632 Great Highway, was built of two retired cable cars, with their front windows, couplings, and holes for kerosene head lamps all intact.

The skeleton of a California Street cable car functions as a jungle gym at Children's Playground in Golden Gate Park. Bottom: Another California Street car, destined for mysterious duty at a street fair in New York City, is wafted eastward with maximum public notice in an American Airlines 747.

Iron Monsters on Market Street

With a rumble and a clang, electric trolleys invaded downtown San Francisco in the 1890s. They were an unwelcome innovation (scarcely anybody likes the look of overhead wires), and they grew even more unpopular when it was disclosed that streetcar companies were passing money to the city supervisors in return for franchises.

The upshot was that the city, in a mood of turn-of-the-century populism, decided to develop its own public utilities, starting with a water system and a municipal railway. Muni cars went into service side by side with those of the Market Street Railway in 1912. The two trolley systems ran competition for thirty-two years before the reluctant Muni was persuaded to swallow the last morsels of its profitless private rival. Then, with a perversity that only government officials could understand, the city proceeded to dismantle the splendid streetcar system it had acquired.

Despite subsequent tree-planting, brick-paving, sign-removal, and sidewalk-widening, Market Street has never been so grand, so well used, or so well regarded as when it was the Champs-Élysées of streetcars, and Iron Monsters wallowed four abreast from the Ferry Building to Twin Peaks Tunnel.

Only the Market Street Railway ran up and down the main stem in 1910, when the picture at left was taken. Sixty-seven years later, the intersection of Fifth and Market (below left) looks remarkably unchanged. Rolling stock, shoppers, and some buildings are new—and the cupola of the Humboldt Bank has been painted red, white, and blue for the Bicentennial—but Muni trolleys still follow the well-worn tracks.

By the early '30s there were four tracks, and iron monsters lumbered along nose-to-tail like a procession of elephants. Market Sheet Railway cars had inside tracks, Muni cars (designated by letters) ran outside. A newspasper used a six-foot man to show that there was only two feet between passing cars. The ubiquitous Mayor James Rolph, Jr., inaugurated the Muni's new B (Geary) line with a platform speech. Everyone loved the streetcars. For five cents you could ride from the bay to the beach. If you were agile and a little daring, you could ride hindside for free.

A 1923 Star carries a payload of twelve newspaper editors, car salesmen, and other expendable bodies up Broadway (above) in a display of nerveless daring. The sleek 1920 Franklin at right gobbles up the cobbles of California Street above Grant Avenue—but, after all, it has only the driver inside.

No Clutch to Slip, No Gears to Strip

When at last motorcars came and hurled themselves at Taylor Street and Twenty-second Street and upper Broadway, it was like the Cairo-to-Cape Town every spring, with Flints and Stars and Studebakers struggling up the cobblestones to claim the easeful mastery of America's most famous urban hills. Manufacturers boiled over with enthusiasm: "Hills don't bother the new 1910 Cartercar," bubbled the Cartercar Company of Pontiac, Michigan. "No clutch to slip, no gears to strip . . ." With twenty-five horsepower and a chain-in-oil drive, the Carter could climb a 50 per cent grade—approximately the pitch of Cheops' pyramid.

All the same, San Francisco officials began to seal off the most challenging (not to say insurmountable) streets, turning them into pedestrian stairways or belvederes, and decreeing that vehicles must be parked with wheels crimped against the curb—or, on the steepest streets, parked perpendicular to the curb. Before long, however, *everyone* was cresting the hills by car, and that took all the fun out of it except for a few Nervous Nellies from the flats of Indiana who can still be heard, descending Mason Street or climbing Powell, softly murmuring, "Wheeee."

Making it to the top always has occasioned a sense of relief in morbidly imaginative drivers. Above, a Studebaker touring car of the early '20s wins glory before an admiring throng. At right, a 1960-ish Volkswagen Bug, unsung, conquers the south face of Nob Hill.

Below: A 1924 Kissel, rejoicing in eight powerful cylinders, breezes up California Street in high gear. Lower right: Perpendicular parking is a safety measure in Pacific Heights, on Russian Hill, and in other areas where a runaway car can be deadly.

The Celebrated Lombard Curlicue

Weary of show-off drivers who delighted in rocketing up and down the steepest hills, city engineers decided in the early 1920s to close off the most precipitous streets, convert a few to ramp-like parks, and barricade others with ornamental balustrades. Their masterpiece was the transformation of a 26 per cent grade on Lombard Street into a sinuous series of banked curves, calculated to thwart the most demonic thrill-seeker. Contractors stripped away the cobblestone slope, poured a series of gracefully winding concrete abutments, and paved the surface with red bricks. John McLaren's park gardeners landscaped the switchbacks with succulent plants: the Lombard zigzag stood as the monument of mind over motorist.

Drivers, naturally, adored it. From opening day, local residents and tourists went out of their way to make the slightly nauseating descent—or ascent, for the street was open in those days to two-way traffic. Car dealers used it to demonstrate new models, neighbors adorned it with hydrangea shrubs, and the city's office of tourism fell helplessly in love with it. Four-color advertisements in national magazines likened Lombard to a ski run. The Chamber of Commerce called it "America's most slithering street," while the Convention and Visitors Bureau, perhaps mindful of another San Francisco street that literally slithered into the sea, hailed it "The Crookedest Street in the World."

Whether or not Lombard Street is the global ultimate in arterial sinuosity is in dispute, but there is no question of its popularity. Postcards showing the curlicue have sold better in recent years than those of any other San Francisco scene.

Rebuilding Lombard Street (top right) between Hyde and Leavenworth Streets in 1922 was meant to curb reckless driving; instead it created today's tourist lure (lower right).

DO
NOT
ENTER

A Pons Asinorum

It was a dream of fools, the non-fools said, pointing out that the notion of bridging the bay (and of extending the span westward to the Farallon Islands) had the official sanction of Joshua Norton, the noted free-lunch scrounger and self-proclaimed Emperor of the United States.

But among the other fools who thought it could be done were the builders of the Central Pacific Railroad, who surveyed, then abandoned, the route more than a century ago; the San Francisco Board of Supervisors, who looked into it a few years later (same outcome); and the wild-eyed maniacs of the Hoover administration, who contrived to put up the requisite $75 million in low-interest federal loans to the State of California in the early 1930s.

The only real fools, it now appears, were those who underestimated the popular appeal of driving to and fro between San Francisco and the East Bay. The bridge, designed to handle 125,000 vehicles a day, reached capacity in 1964 and has been, so to speak, oversubscribed ever since. Tolls paid off the cost of the project and now help support other bridges and the money-losing Bay Area Rapid Transit system, which was supposed to reduce commuter traffic on the Bay Bridge—and has, by about 2 per cent.

Between twenty and thirty thousand motorists got out of their cars, prowled around, peered over the rail, and shared coffee while westbound vehicles stood still for more than two hours on a Saturday afternoon in January 1975. A year earlier there had been real *congestion when 150 cars were wrecked, stalled, or abandoned during a rain-soaked, all-night tie-up. Amiable toll takers (this young woman among them) give words of comfort, but during the evening rush the only happy drivers are those who are headed against the crowd.*

Not yet a span, the cantilevered east section creeps toward Yerba Buena Island late in 1934 to join the suspension bridge to the west and give the lie to skeptics who said that tides were too swift, the bottom too soft, and the bay too wide to be bridged. The curved pier in the foregound is the Key System ferry mole.

Girders that would support two decks dangled from steel cables in 1935 as the bridge neared completion. In a classic view at far right (west from Yerba Buena Island) the upper deck is serving two-way auto traffic, while the lower deck handles trucks and commuter trains. All vehicles now use the upper deck westbound, the lower eastbound—and BART trains run under the bay.

The Great Bay Area Electric Train Caper

Nobody but the owners had much praise for Key Route's seventy-five-mile, three-county system of electric trains and connecting ferryboats during its years of power and profit, strikes and receivership from 1903 to 1958. However, since the completion in 1974, at a cost of $1.3 billion, of the Bay Area Rapid Transit District's seventy-five-mile, three-county system of electric trains over substantially the same route, plaintive voices have been heard crying, "Why on earth did we let them scrap the Key?"

Francis Marion Smith, who did so well mining sodium tetraborate in Death Valley that he was known ever after as "Borax" Smith, put together the Key Route out of assorted East Bay streetcar companies and short-line railroads. Various county supervisors, state legislators, realtors, merchants, public relations folk, and engineers put together BART out of thin air and the biggest public bond issue in history. So far as anyone remembers, there was never an option to keep Key: it simply was swallowed up in A-C Transit, a publicly owned East Bay bus system that is still in operation and doing fine.

An eight-car Key System train with a payload of Piedmonters heads west on Fortieth Street at Broadway, Oakland, on a morning in the '30s. The diamond-shaped pantographs on the roofs picked up electricity from overhead wires. When trains later crossed the bridge, they took power from an electrified rail.

Elegance above the tracks: the Tudor-style Key Route Inn, at Twenty-second Street and Broadway in Oakland, straddled the B line. Built by "Borax" Smith in 1906, the inn burned to the ground in 1932.

A Key Route train crosses the rattling 3.5-mile wooden trestle to ferryboat slips at the Oakland Mole in the 1920s (top left). From 1939 to 1958, electric trains ran on the lower deck of the Bay Bridge. BART trains (above and left) glide along the center of freeways and burrow under the bay in a double-track tube, 3.6 miles long and as much as 135 feet below the bay's surface.

Commuters at the Oakland Mole in the 1930s trudge from a Southern Pacific ferry to a Key Route train (below left). Commuters at San Francisco's Montgomery Street station in the 1970s line up at the doorway of a BART train to Fremont in Alameda County.

The mile-wide Golden Gate as it looked in 1900 (top), when only madmen and visionaries talked of bridging the strait, and (center) as it would have looked if bridged as chief engineer Joseph B. Strauss and city engineer Michael O'Shaughnessy proposed in 1921. Strauss designed this monster—part suspension, part cantilever—because he, too, thought the gap was too great for a single span. Right: The bridge from Covallo Point on the Marin County shore. Opposite page, top: Four lanes of traffic push north at twilight. Two center lanes are reversed to carry morning commuters southbound into the city.

A Praiseworthy Project

So much has been written in praise of the Golden Gate Bridge, its beauty, its daring, and the skill of its engineers, and so much in dispraise of the Golden Gate Bridge, Highway, and Transportation District, which runs it, that the authors beg leave to avoid hyperbole and to present instead some little-known facts and figures on this widely known structure.

- Age of bridge: 43 on May 27, 1980 (Gemini).
- Cost of bridge: $74 million, of which more than half was interest paid to persons who thoughtfully bought bridge revenue bonds during the Depression.
- Age of Golden Gate: roughly 25,000 years. Earlier, it was a river connecting a valley to the ocean.
- Other name for Golden Gate: Chrysopylae, a term seldom used to describe the bridge in polite company.
- Length of suspended span: 77,400 inches.
- Reason for orange color: to avoid confusion with other bridges of the same or similar name.
- Favorite vehicle in which to cross bridge: car.
- Favorite hour at which to cross bridge: 5 P.M.
- Weight of towers: 88,800,000 pounds—as much as 100,000 men weighing 888 pounds each.

Hangars and apron hugged the Bayshore Highway in October 1928 (top). In the 1940s the city paid $1,250,000 to reroute a state freeway, opening five hundred acres for runways, parking, new terminals, and service facilities. In 1968 the main terminal (bottom) was already outgrown.

The Little Mudhole That Could

Down on the bayside tide flats of the Ogden Mills estate, several miles south of the San Mateo County line, a team of surveyors set up their tripod one morning late in 1926 and measured out a couple of runways, 200 feet wide and 1,850 feet long, the city's first public commitment to aviation. With its usual mixture of high ambition and parochial jealousy, San Francisco had turned down a site in Alameda County in favor of a lone venture on its "own" side of the bay.

For decades it looked as if the choice was the worst mistake since the gridiron street plat. In the first two years, three mail carriers moved out to escape the fog. Voters turned down improvement bond issues. Year after year, the field lost money. Charles Lindbergh, the world's most renowned pilot, caught the wheels of a passenger plane in blue clay along one of the runways. "It's a mudhole," one aviator said. "Just a mudhole."

During and after World War II, air transportation caught up with Mills Field, or vice versa. Now called San Francisco International, the airport covers five thousand acres, serves twenty-six scheduled and commuter airlines, handles close to twenty million passengers a year. (In the United States, only Chicago, Atlanta, Los Angeles, and New York's J. F. Kennedy are busier.) Thanks largely to revenues from parking, SFO has been self-supporting for almost twenty years.

Top: Plane Park at Mills Field, south of San Francisco, was a lumpy pasture on May 7, 1927, when boxy biplanes flew in for dedication ceremonies. The clapboard terminal (center) housed a waiting room, offices, restrooms, mail room, weather station, radio shack, and living quarters for employees. During its first year it handled fewer than three thousands flights carrying only 4,500 passengers. Today's Central Terminal (below), built from 1951 to 1954 for $6 million, reached capacity in six years and is now flanked by two more terminals and an expanded garage.

SOUTH END RO WING CLUB
END
HYDE
NOT A
THROUGH
STREET

CHAPTER 5

The Joys and Pains of a Diverse Society

A century and a quarter ago, when most American cities were as homogeneous as mayonnaise, the raw young town of San Francisco was drawing population from Canton and Sydney, Munich and Valparaiso. Since then, we have been called, at separate moments of our brief existence, the continent's most Irish, most Italian, most Chinese, most Chileno, most Catholic, most unionized, most alcoholic, most hippie, most homosexual city, the one with the most New Yorkers outside New York, the most Southerners outside the South, the most Tasmanians outside Van Diemen's Land. If these superlatives are not sufficient, let it be known that we harbor significant numbers of Samoans, Maltese, Russian *malakans,* Sikhs, Koreans, Filipinos, San Salvadoreans, Basques, Armenians, vegetarians, Vedantists, Swedenborgians, transsexuals, spiritualists, anarchists, and single-taxers.

This motley mix got started because of the gold rush and has been perpetuated out of habit. We live together because we are here—not necessarily liking one another, but getting along day by day. What has sometimes mistakenly been praised as tolerance is really only laxity. Just as we are too indolent to enforce traffic laws and clean the sidewalks, we are too lazy to enforce conformity.

Word has got around that you can get away with *anything* in San Francisco, and we consequently are compelled to go on living with others who are younger, older, lighter, darker, louder, and more or less messy than ourselves; who hold with devil worship, popery, anabaptism, and astrology; who do strange things to one another after dark; and who have peculiar tastes in food and clothing.

In a world that tends increasingly to sort itself out by color, age, habit of mind, and auto-da-fé, it probably is not a bad idea to live in such imposed diversity. It is possible, of course, to go on hating people who live next door or who sit in an adjoining seat on the bus, but it is tiring to do so and can be dangerous. Most such hatreds finally burn out from sheer exhaustion.

Rich variety in race and language, amusements and styles of life delights most San Franciscans but deeply disturbs those who crave stability. Aquatic Park on a Sunday afternoon (left) serves up clowns, chamber music, sermons, propositions, and pornographic newspapers. A century ago Irish hoodlums (below left) dealt with cultural differences by systematic persecution. Beneath the antagonism lay economic rivalry that culminated in anti-Chinese riots and laws against Asian immigration. Below right: The late Dr. Charles Ertola, an Italian-American Protestant and president of the Board of Supervisors, crowns Miss Chinatown, 1960. The symbolism was not lost on either party.

"HOODLUMS."

Getting Started Together

"The school was in a small rented house planted in the middle of a sandbank on the corner of First and Folsom Streets . . . There was neither a blackboard nor map. The only apparatus consisted of a wooden water pail and a battered tin dipper, from which the children drank water brought from a well not far distant, the owner of which allowed the boys to draw one bucket of water a day . . ."

The writer was John Swett, one of the first school principals in San Francisco and later the state's superintendent of public instruction. The institution where he labored in happy assurance that schooling would "Americanize" the polyglot people of California was the Rincon School, which, if it still existed, would be struggling today with roughly the same task—teaching essentials to children of widely differing cultural and racial backgrounds.

No other American city has faced such diversities in its recent efforts to end racial grouping and to give every pupil equal education. The school district's plan of integration, effected in 1971 under orders from a federal court, required that every elementary school have a proper proportion not only of blacks and whites, but also of Chinese, Japanese, Filipinos, American Indians, and Spanish-surname students.

That this meticulously contrived integration would soon be out of balance was inevitable in a changing city; that the effort to integrate continues, despite discouragement and opposition, is evidence of the legal and political sway of new ideals over old habits.

A precocious display of patriotism at the Golden Gate Kindergarten in the prewar excitement of 1913 brings approving smiles from the teachers, although one young militant has to instruct the boy behind her on how to stand at attention. Lower left: The new generation at an elementary school in the Richmond District streams in from recess on a morning in the late 1970s.

Upper right: Combined glee clubs of Crocker, Hearst, and John Swett Grammar Schools warble favorite melodies of 1910 under the direction of Estelle Carpenter. Center right: French choir of Notre Dame de Victoires School sings the contemporary "Bal de Paris" at a hotel on Union Square.

Going to school in Chinatown at the turn of the century, as depicted in Arnold Genthe's charming photograph (below), was a game of follow-the-leader. In the '70s it is like going to school anywhere—textbooks, uniforms, a meeting place of races and cultures.

T'ang Yen Gai—the Chinese Street

The Chinese have been part of San Francisco since before the gold rush, but their story is shadowed by sorrow, and its beginnings are lost in the self-imposed silence of a proud people who found themselves a rejected and despised minority in a new land.

"There is no Chinese-American history from our own point of view," the Asian-American dramatist Frank Chin has written. "Silence has been part of the price of our survival in a country we knew hated us."

Many of the early immigrants—gold miners, fishermen, laborers on the transcontinental railroad—regarded themselves as visitors, maintaining their Chinese identity in the expectation of eventually returning to China. Their appearance, their language, their competitive energy, their protective cloak of cultural superiority made them easy targets of racial hatred. The exploitation and exclusion of the Chinese in the nineteenth century is the ugliest chapter in San Francisco's history, and it is not over. Although there are now eighty thousand to a hundred thousand Chinese in the city, and old Chinatown has burst its historic boundaries, the Asian community remains isolated from much of the city's economic, political, and cultural life.

Old Chinatown's Street of Gamblers (upper left) around the turn of the century, in a famous photograph by Arnold Genthe. The Chinatown of today (above) resembles the old in one major respect: it is still a racial ghetto.

Shopping on the Street of the Men of China a hundred years ago (far left) and today (below)—always a dependable place to buy winter melons, pork dumplings, dried duck, and the spices of a unique and exacting cuisine.

Wall newspapers in Spofford Alley, 1889 (below). To some whites, Chinese garments signaled a refusal to "acculturate." Wall newspapers of today (above) are a community tradition that has survived political change, ideological upheaval, and a change of costume.

Shaking Hands with the Dragon

For more than a century, during all the years of blind, anti-Chinese prejudice that finally melted into guilty, exaggerated admiration, white tourists have been snooping around in Chinatown. In the 1870s, Caucasian "inspectors" guided visitors from New York and Boston to opium dens, gambling hells, and (on the deluxe tour) the lair of a musician who played "There'll Be a Hot Time in the Old Town Tonight" on a two-stringed Asian violin.

To be the object of touristic curiosity—even of a sentimental, racist love affair—never has compensated Chinese-Americans for decades of discriminatory legislation, legal oppression, and social ostracism—but it has produced millions in revenue for the trinket shops and chow mein refectories of Grant Avenue.

New Year's dragon dance on Grant Avenue (below) runs a gauntlet of spectators and fusillades of firecrackers, draws an estimated 250,000 to Chinatown each winter. In Oakland in 1907 (bottom right) the whole affair was less exuberant, less populous, and less profitable.

Along the tourist route a "charming child" welcomes the day's contingent from Boston into her father's shop in the 1870s (left). The man in a derby presumably is Captain O'Neil, Detective Avon, or another of the Old Chinatown Hands. Right: A touristic museum now displays the celebrated dragon year round.

Japanese musicians in kimonos enchanted audiences at Woodward's Gardens in the 1860s, as at a festival in the 1970s (far right). During the years between, Japanese have suffered persecution, discriminatory legislation, and loss of liberty and property.

A New Song on an Old Samisen

Of all the particles in San Francisco's mosaic of races, the Japanese have experienced the most numerous and unpredictable changes of fortune. Like the Chinese, they at first impressed white residents as a charming curiosity—an aloof, industrious people whose looks and habits marked them as indigestibly exotic. Unlike the Chinese, they did not immediately run into discrimination: they were too few to cause hostility. It was only in the 1890s, when thousands of Japanese workers began arriving on the West Coast by way of Hawaii, that an outcry arose from trade unions, small businessmen, farmers, and native son clubs. The federal government pressured Japan into a diplomatic agreement

Confusion, bitterness, and fear followed U. S. Executive Order 9066 in February 1942, authorizing removal of Japanese from "military areas" to inland camps. Photographs by Dorothea Lange eloquently record the humiliation of this imprisonment.

Japanese culture, back in style, draws tourists to festivals in San Francisco's new Japantown, centered around a Peace Plaza.

to stop the "yellow tide," as the papers were calling it, and later passed laws to prevent Japanese from owning land or immigrating into the United States.

The nadir came just after the Japanese attack on Hawaii, when many Californians, fearful and furious, became convinced that Japanese farmers, fishermen, and gardeners were awaiting only a signal from the emperor to seize control of the Pacific states. The Government removed 110,000 coastal residents of Japanese heritage—more than two thirds of them American-born—to concentration camps in remote desert areas.

No less remarkable than this fit of hysteria was its postwar reaction. San Franciscans led the country in embracing Japanese styles and products and drew Japanese-Americans into such warm social integration that a group of Japanese community leaders complained not long ago that their people in northern California were losing cultural and political identity.

"New Nippon" brought street front commerce and aromas of seaweed and dried shrimp to Geary and Buchanan Streets a few months after the great fire. Hostesses in nearby Pacific Heights were delighted to hire a "Frank," as all Japanese houseboys were called, at thirty-five cents an hour With White Coat, twenty-five cents an hour Without.

A Tale of the Nihonmachi

Late arrivals in a crowded city, some ten thousand Japanese huddled on the fringe of Chinatown until the 1906 earthquake-fire destroyed their homes along Bush, Pine, and Sutter Streets just west of Kearny. While the Chinese were rebuilding their traditional neighborhood, the Japanese moved like one big, restless family out to the Western Addition, where rows of Gothic mansions had escaped the fire. It was a fine time to buy real estate in a frightened city. Caucasian residents greeted the newcomers by moving to San Mateo. (The notion of integrated settlements had few enthusiasts at the time—besides, the area appeared to be going commercial.)

A tidy if eclectic Japantown grew up along California, Geary, and O'Farrell Streets between Franklin and Webster: Buddhist temples in three-story row houses, fish markets in the gardens of Italianate mansions, sukiyaki restaurants in basements on Buchanan Street.

It was this neighborhood of San Francisco that the Japanese were forced to abandon during the internment in World War II and that they were determined to reclaim, despite a major redevelopment along Geary. The city agreed to set aside three blocks for a Japanese Trade and Cultural Center; Japanese investors built a hotel, a kabuki theater, and a bridge of shops arching over Fillmore Street—all white mortar and teak beams, quite unlike the strange accumulation of bay windows, wooden cornices, and hand-painted ideograms, white-on-black, that had characterized the old Japantown.

Some Japanese decry this commercialization, this touristic exploitation of a residential district that is, in truth, a racial ghetto. To outsiders, the new Nihonmachi shows evidence of the strength of a generation of Japanese-Americans emerging physically and spiritually out of the privacy of their quiet ethnic slum.

Japan Center offers fans and lanterns, rice cakes, tempura, and a Japanese hotel overlooking a five-tiered Peace Pagoda, a gift from the people of Japan. An almost continuous display of karate, judo, fencing, and dancing lures Caucasian tourists and keeps three hundred thousand Japanese visitors a year from feeling homesick.

Fading Images of an Italian Village

Fifty years ago, when Italian immigration into California reached its peak, the long diagonal of Columbus Avenue, rising from Montgomery Street to Broadway, then flowing gently down through North Beach to the bay, was known accurately as Little Italy.

There is no Little Italy today, not in the form of a compact linguistic and cultural ghetto. The Italians left it behind when they moved out into every social and cultural and economic level of California, impressing their names on business and politics, athletics and arts: Angelotti, Apostoli, DiMaggio, Giannini, Merola, Belgrano, Fontana, Coppola, DiGiorgio, Ricci, Alioto, Sbarbaro, Pierotti, Belli, Zirpoli.

But vestiges of the immigrant separatism, the peninsular pride, persist in this most Mediterranean of neighborhoods, manifested by the aging pioneers who have remained and by the institutions that tied them to the homeland and to one another—the Italian churches, the import groceries, the caffè espresso bars, the spaghetti factories, the travel agencies, the restaurants, the clubs. One by one, the old immigrants are disappearing, like the styles they brought from Genova and Lucca and Palermo. Little Italy becomes a figment of the mind, celebrated on Columbus Day and then forgotten, crumbling under the peaceful but relentless pressure of the Chinese, flowing north and eastward, down Nob Hill: the newer Americans.

The late George Moscone, San Francisco's third mayor of Italian ancestry, joined Christopher Columbus (Joseph Cervetto) at Aquatic Park for the annual re-enactment of the navigator's landing in the New World. Columbus Day, a major celebration in Northern California, occasions two weeks of banquets, processions, and congratulatory advertising.

Saints Peter and Paul (1923), "the marzipan church" to poet Lawrence Ferlinghetti, quaintly blends Gothic, Romanesque, and Local Ingenuity. Each October since the mid-1930s, a society of parishioners has paraded a painting of the Madonna del Lume (below), patron of Sicilian seafarers, from the sanctuary on Washington Square to Fisherman's Wharf, where a priest blesses the fleet.

The ancient bowling game of bocce ball, played by older Italians every day at Aquatic Park, becomes a tournament of ethnic skill during the Columbus festival. Italian-Americans also compete in a regatta, softball, soccer, golf, and liar's dice.

Pressing out an 1890s vintage at a community vat on Telegraph Hill, Italian wine-makers brought Old World skills to California vines.

With two full bottles per man—one red, one white—diners at a fraternal mixer in North Beach in 1912 sampled products of Italian enterprise—a foretaste of today's Gallo, Petri, Parducci, Franzia, Mondavi, Martini, Cribari, Sebastiani, and Italian-Swiss.

Marches, Mobs, and Manifestos

Do we really have a predilection for communal violence out here at the western limit of sanity—or does it only seem that we do?

The two Americans who have written most sensibly on the peculiarities of Californian life, Josiah Royce and Carey McWilliams, both discerned a habit of dissent attributable to our frontier diversity. Professor Royce, writing fifty years after the American conquest of Mexican California, observed that two traits of character repeatedly had disrupted social order: a general irresponsibility, typical of any crowd of strangers; and a "diseased" exaggeration of the common American contempt for foreigners. McWilliams, who hailed his native state on its hundredth birthday as "The Great Exception," concluded that the one certainty about California was that everything runs to extremes. In the British view of Lord Bryce, a curious observer of San Francisco's anti-Chinese riots in the late 1870s, it was a passion for speculation that had "bred a recklessness and turbulence in the inner life of the [San Franciscan] which does not fail to express itself in acts."

No, it cannot be denied. We *do* have a certain tendency, ambiguous in origin, unpredictable in form: A century and a quarter after the Vigilantes of the 1850s cleverly used mob violence as a solution to the problem of mob violence, we *do* tend to carry signs and clubs, bullhorns and gas bombs, in preference to the tedious ways of courts and parliaments.

A funeral in the aftermath of violence (above) drew a mile-long column of union sympathizers to Steuart Street, near the unfinished Bay Bridge, in July 1934, to mourn two strikers killed on the waterfront. In July 1856 (lower left) nobody regretted Joseph Hetherington and Philander Brace, a couple of undistinguished murderers singled out for exemplary sacrifice by the Committee of Vigilance, but thousands of self-appointed regenerators, having seized control of the city, showed up for the open-air hanging at Davis and Sacramento Streets.

Vice President Nelson Rockefeller, speaking inside a nearby hotel, was the putative object of this organized disapproval in October 1974, but the pickets clearly were more interested in chanting, chatting, and poaching on the wrought iron fence of the Pacific Union Club. The peaceable rally (right) in Golden Gate Park in the autumn of 1969 called for an end to the Vietnam War. The marchers below, suffused with love for fresh air, creative haberdashery, and the United Farm Workers, are en route to an afternoon of dissidence at Dolores Park.

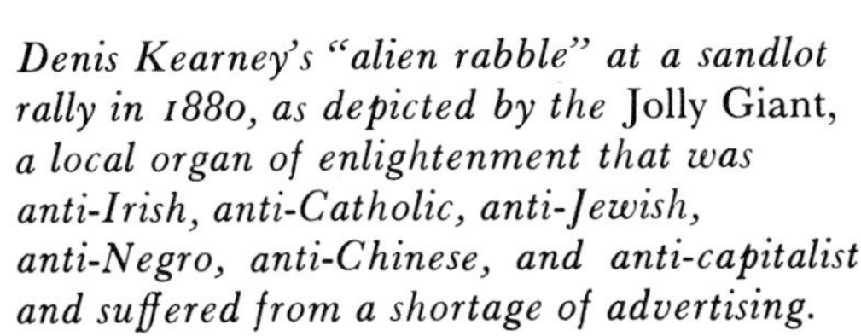

Denis Kearney's "alien rabble" at a sandlot rally in 1880, as depicted by the Jolly Giant, *a local organ of enlightenment that was anti-Irish, anti-Catholic, anti-Jewish, anti-Negro, anti-Chinese, and anti-capitalist and suffered from a shortage of advertising.*

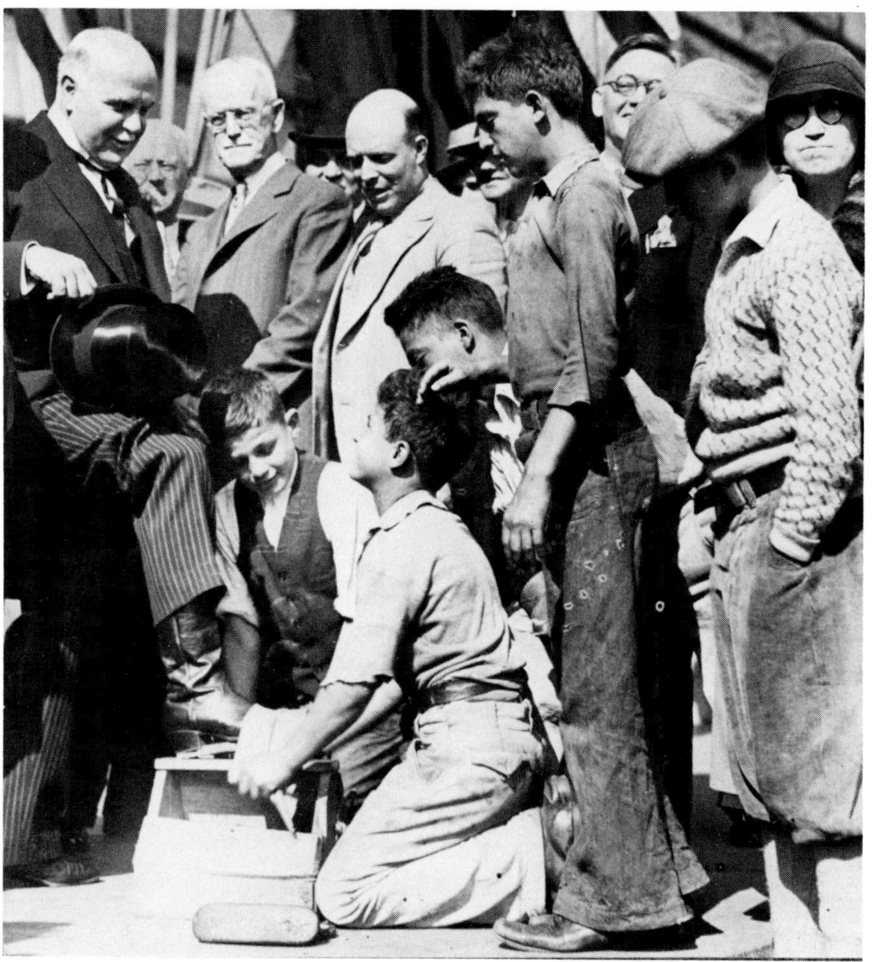

Frisco flamboyance (1912–31) was personified in James "Sunny Jim" Rolph, Jr., whose top hat, striped pants, cutaway, and cowboy boots set the tone for an expansive, gregarious decade. Most popular of all mayors, Rolph was re-elected four times, could have been crowned grand duke had he not become governor, a job in which he died, a failure, in 1934.

Savoir flair (1966–73), an irrepressible tongue, and a Medicean taste for the arts endeared Joseph L. Alioto to reporters and cameramen. The romance died when the talents of the wealthy anti-trust lawyer turned to campaigns for higher office, feuds with local columnists, aborted building projects, and litigation to defend his prior professional activities and to win a libel suit against a magazine that had falsely linked him to the Mafia.

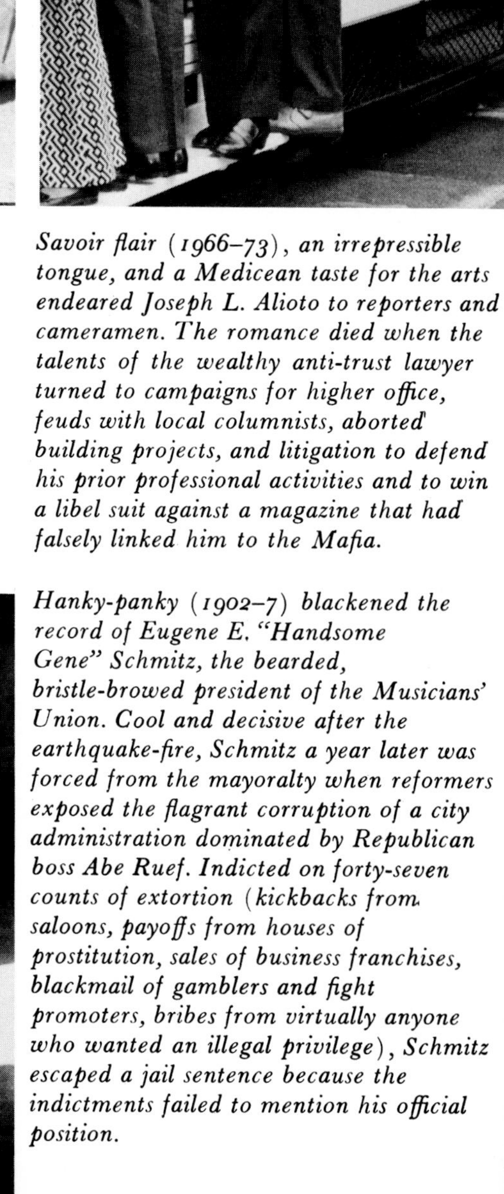

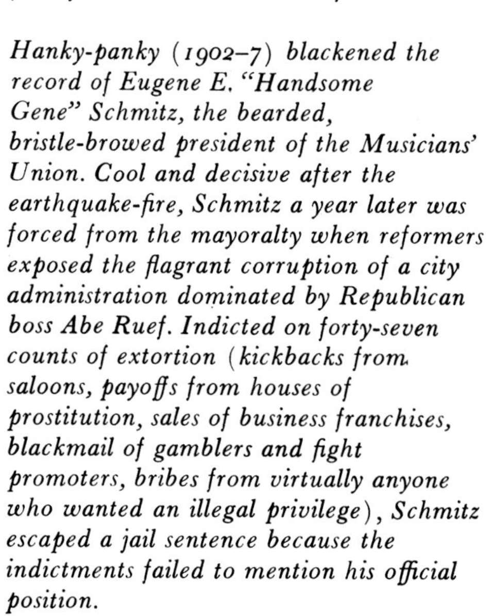

Hanky-panky (1902–7) blackened the record of Eugene E. "Handsome Gene" Schmitz, the bearded, bristle-browed president of the Musicians' Union. Cool and decisive after the earthquake-fire, Schmitz a year later was forced from the mayoralty when reformers exposed the flagrant corruption of a city administration dominated by Republican boss Abe Ruef. Indicted on forty-seven counts of extortion (kickbacks from saloons, payoffs from houses of prostitution, sales of business franchises, blackmail of gamblers and fight promoters, bribes from virtually anyone who wanted an illegal privilege), Schmitz escaped a jail sentence because the indictments failed to mention his official position.

Mayors Major and Minor

San Francisco's first mayor (or *alcalde,* to be precise) was a middle-aged rancher named Francisco de Haro, an exemplary citizen who had come north as a sublieutenant in the Mexican Army, laid out the first street in the pueblo of Yerba Buena in 1835, served in various civic and military capacities for more than twenty years, and died grieving his twin sons, killed by Yankee insurrectionists in one of the few fatal encounters in the American annexation of California.

Lately, most of our mayors have been lawyers (Tocqueville was right about the lawyer aristocracy); but in between there have been thirty-five, thirty-six, or fifty-three widely assorted types (the total depends on whether you count repeaters, alcaldes, and short-term fill-ins). Among them were: a twenty-four-year-old barber (Juan Nepomuceno Padilla, 1844–45, who confessed after a couple of months in office that he was hopelessly incompetent and also wanted to leave for Sonoma); an Army chaplain (Thaddeus M. Leavenworth, 1848); a Mississippi riverboat captain in the employ of Commodore Vanderbilt (Cornelius K. Garrison, 1853–54); a produce merchant (Edward M. Pond, 1887–90); an attorney-physician-poet (Dr. Edward R. Taylor, 1907–10); and a florist (Angelo J. Rossi, 1932–43).

Late in 1978, Dianne Feinstein, the first woman to hold the mayoral office, was elected by her fellow-members of the Board of Supervisors to serve out the term of George Moscone (1975–78), who was shot and killed at City Hall, allegedly by a former supervisor who had come to plead for political patronage.

Noblesse oblige (1895–97) rested comfortably on Adolph Sutro, a patrician liberal who made millions boring a tunnel to drain water from Nevada mines and at one time owned a tenth of San Francisco. Sutro lectured local legislators in his German accent on the evils of bosses, party influence, and greedy railroads, made gifts to the city of parks, pools, and performances of Shakespeare at his seaside mansion, where the barking of sea lions competed with the musings of Hamlet.

Fighting words and wild shots (1880–81) rocketed the Rev. Isaac S. Kalloch, a strapping red-haired evangelist (known enviously as "The Sorrel Stallion"), into the mayoral office during a period of radical, sandlot politics. Chronicle *publisher Charles de Young (with inflammatory sheet in hand) aired Kalloch's record of "adulterous amours"; the Stallion retorted with a slanderous sermon on the de Young family tree; and de Young countered by gunning down Kalloch at the nearest street corner. As a wounded hero, Kalloch was elected to one undistinguished term, but in 1880 his unforgiving son stormed in the* Chronicle *city room and murdered Charles de Young.*

Women voted here for the first time in March 1912. Only 30 per cent of eligible voters, including four thousand females, turned out for the municipal election, but they made their mark by approving bonds to build the Civic Center, an $8.8 million bargain that included City Hall, the Auditorium, and the Main Library. One woman complained that an officer at her precinct impudently addressed her by her first name as she left; otherwise women's suffrage began and has continued without rancor.

Letting the People Decide

Sunny Jim Rolph, our most influential mayor, had an amiable solution to every policy dispute that gummed up city government: "Let the people decide."

In Rolph's time "the people" were more homogeneous than they are today, more likely to be influenced by the advice of the downtown business community; but the idea of tossing decisions to the voters has taken such a strong hold in San Francisco that it has grown into an obsession, producing dozens of complicated local measures on every election ballot.

Time was, we had no such zest for popular opinion. At our first election under American command in 1846, the only question was whether or not to confirm the appointment of a young Navy lieutenant, Washington Allen Bartlett, who had been tapped by his captain to act as alcalde of the village. The ballot box was an empty crate that had held flasks of lemon syrup. Bartlett got sixty-six votes; his chief opponent, Bob Ridley, the pool hall keeper, got twenty-six; and Nate Spear, part-owner of the general store, got one. Nobody asked for a recount.

Contrast this Arcadian choosing process with the municipal ballot of 1948, when the busy voters passed judgment on forty-two amendments to the city charter. Or with 1977, when 117 candidates ran for 11 seats on the Board of Supervisors (equivalent to city council) and the ballot measures stretched from A to V.

Clearly, the city has grown in more than size. If ballot democracy is a virtue, we are with the angels. But, when decisions are too numerous, it is difficult to discern which ones are important. That's the trouble with letting the people decide.

A bearded decision-maker punches a computer card at a poll in the basement of police headquarters during city elections in 1977. Voting by districts for the first time since the 1920s, the people decided that the Board of Supervisors should have its first elected Asian member, its first black female, and its largest-ever proportion of women (three out of eleven). Below: Ethnic trends affect campaigning in North Beach.

The presidential election of 1896 brought long queues to a booth in Chinatown. That evening, when the Chronicle signaled returns from the East with blinking lights on its tower at Kearny and Market, continuous red flashes announced the victory of Republican William McKinley over Democrat William Jennings Bryan. But the city chose a Democratic mayor, young millionaire James D. Phelan, Jr. Below: The moment of reckoning at a precinct in the lobby of the St. Francis Hotel in 1952. The decision went to Dwight D. Eisenhower over Adlai Stevenson.

Making the Street Scene

Jesus Christ Satan stopped in at a meeting of the Finance Committee of the Board of Supervisors a couple of years ago. He was barefoot, as usual, with a Japanese fan in hand, his face streaked with white greasepaint and dotted with azure sequins, a United Nations flag around his shoulders, a Pomeranian under one arm and a drooping bouquet of marigolds under the other.

"I've come to tell you to throw open your prisons, forgive all criminals," Mr. Satan said, while the chairman yawned discreetly against his knuckles. "That's what I'm going to do when I'm elected."

Mr. Satan was not elected, but he was photographed and interviewed by the *Chronicle*. That set him up considerably while making his daily rounds of Montgomery Street, wearing a feathered hat and whacking a tambourine. It confirmed his status as a Public Character in a crowded field that reaches back more than a century to the happy reign of Norton I, Emperor of the United States and Protector of Mexico.

Nobody ever questioned Norton's standing. His royal scrip was honored in bars and restaurants, and his dogs, Bummer and Lazarus, had an official freedom of the city. His successors, less renowned, found niches in our local pantheon: Freddie Coombs, whose view of himself was mingled

with the person of George Washington; the Guttersnipe, who mined curbstones; Tiny Armstrong, who sweetened the air of Union Square with his bird whistles and cries of "Hello, honey, you look *gorgeous* today!"

But the breed has got out of control. So many amiable madmen and crazy foxes crowd the streets that it is difficult to tell a mercenary entertainer from a noble mendicant. Nowadays, a crackpot has to hire a P.R. person and run for office to rate a mention in a book.

A modern Diogenes stops passers-by on Powell Street. The question remains, did he find what he was searching for?

NATIONAL MARITIME MUSEUM AT SAN FRANCISCO

Rushing to settle accounts before the departure of a steamer for the East, the city's best-known borrowers and lenders throng banks and shipping agencies in a cartoon by Ed Jump (1866). John Wieland, the brewer, carries hatboxes and a carpetbag; banker Michael Reese (in checked suit) clutches a poke of money; while Emperor Norton (center front) turns out an empty pocket for the inspection of Sheriff J. S. Ellis.

Costumed representatives of God and Mammon, art and entertainment, station themselves on downtown corners. The chick advertises business machinery on Montgomery Street; the ballerina and friends solicit contributions to the San Francisco Ballet.

Neatly pruned street trees—a rarity then as now—gave a European look to the Gothic castle of furniture manufacturer Nathaniel P. Cole at the northwest corner of Franklin and Sacramento Streets, in 1887.

Louis Schwabacher, whose family has long been prominent in West Coast business, decreed a fortress tower, a filigree widow's walk, and stylish wooden stalactites on his new house (1888) on Clay Street near Gough.

Michael H. de Young, publisher of the Chronicle, *built this bide-a-wee at 1919 California Street in the early 1880s to house his future family, later the Mesdames Joseph O. Tobin, Ferdinand Theriot, George Cameron, and Nion Tucker.*

The Charles Crockers (he was the contractor member of the Central Pacific's Big Four) bedded down baronially on the north side of California Street between Taylor and Jones, now the site of Grace Cathedral.

CHAPTER 6

Cherished Relics of a Robust Past

Measured by the standards of Europe, Asia, or the eastern shores of North America, the story of San Francisco is ridiculously short. Spanish priests and soldiers founded a mission and an army post on the edge of the bay in 1776, but it was not until the 1830s, after Mexico had established her independence, that the settlement became a town, and not until 1847, after the United States took over the province of Upper California, that this cluster of mud-brick shanties took the name San Francisco, which previously had belonged to only the bay.

Perhaps it is the very brevity of local history that gives San Franciscans a peculiar outlook toward things past—an ambivalent mixture of pride and indifference. To the amusement of outsiders, San Franciscans can work up a civic commotion over some landmark of questionable appearance and negligible antiquity, while at the same time accepting the destruction of whole neighborhoods, traditions, and institutions to the expediencies of economics or technology.

For the past decade or two, preservation has been in fashion. Now, the city self-consciously catalogues its souvenirs—precious little heaps of wood and mortar from the epoch of Hispanic colonization, from the gold rush, the Nevada silver boom, the expositions, the earthquake, the fire.

But the preservation cult came late. Our beloved remains are few. From the era of exploration—nothing. From the half century of Spanish and Mexican occupation, only the Franciscan mission and the much-remodeled Officers' Mess at the Presidio. From the gold rush, a few brick storefronts and the hulls of sunken ships beneath the downtown streets. Out of all the stately nineteenth-century residences on these pages, only the Haas-Lilienthal house (below) at 2007 Franklin Street, remains, providing a destination for tourists, a center for receptions, and an appropriate office for the Foundation for San Francisco's Architectural Heritage. The others, like their occupants in the 1880s, have gone to dust.

A Brassy Calling Card from an English Visitor

Golden Hinde II, *a $1.5 million reproduction of a three-masted British galleon, sailed into San Francisco Bay in March 1975 after a thirteen-thousand mile-journey from England. Built as a tourist attraction, GH II was temporarily moored near Fisherman's Wharf, then sailed off to become a movie set.*

That Captain Francis Drake—Mayor of Plymouth, servant of the queen, and despoiler of the Spanish Main—landed his galleon *Golden Hinde* somewhere in or near San Francisco Bay on a June day in 1579 and claimed the territory for Elizabeth I is an undisputed fact. Beyond that, almost everything about Drake's visit is a historic puzzle of the sort that leads to pamphleteering, exchanges of articles in scholarly journals, and ruined friendships.

Controversy focuses on whether Drake entered the bay or bypassed the fogbound Golden Gate to land farther north. Discovery of a five by eight-inch brass marker (shown in a rubbing below) inside the Gate raised more doubts than it resolved. When a 102-foot modern reproduction of a ship resembling Drake's wooden galleon arrived in California several years ago, it, too, ran into strife. Karl Kortum, director of the San Francisco Maritime Museum, called the vessel "Ye Olde Tourist Trappe," and the owners retaliated with a suit for $500,000 damages. Meanwhile, as the state government quietly made plans to commemorate the four-hundredth anniversary of Drake's landing, historians at the University of California sheepishly admitted that the brass plaque they had displayed for forty years had turned out to be a clever fake.

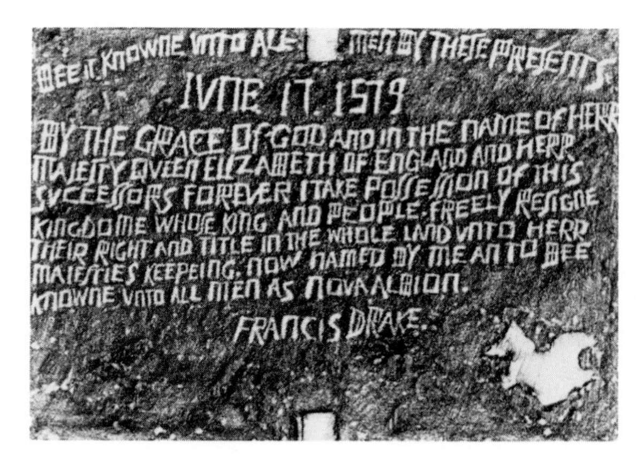

A brass plaque with an Elizabethan inscription, found at Point San Quentin, inside the bay, in 1936, seemed to settle the question of Drake's landing place until a chauffeur testified that he had found the plate three years earlier "near Drake's Bay." Historians authenticated the relic, however, and put it on display at the University of California. Only in 1977 did the director of U.C.'s Bancroft Library announce that further tests had proved the plate a fraud. It was old metal, worked into a deceptive design by a prankster. Left: A seventeenth-century Dutch print shows native Californians crowning Drake as thousands cheer. Authenticity of this picture is not in question. It's pure fantasy.

While fifty thousand spectators crowded the shore, thousands of small craft escorted Golden Hinde II *through the strait that Drake may have missed in the fog. When shore batteries fired* two *twenty-one gun salutes, the captain of the fifteen-man British crew murmured, "Really!"*

Drake's Estero, thirty-seven miles north of the Golden Gate on the south shore of Point Reyes, is, according to many historians, where Drake landed to repair his ship. Others argue the case for Bolinas lagoon or for Point San Quentin, inside San Francisco Bay.

The Land They Found

The Spanish cavalry officers who explored and colonized the coast of California occupy a curious niche in San Francisco's gallery of historic icons. All of them are remembered: their names adorn streets and schools, suburbs and housing tracts. But their separate souls, their agonies, their wild surmises have congealed into a single, anonymous figure—the conquistador. Mounted on a silver saddle, wrapped in a sable cloak, topped with a broad, three-cornered hat, he emerges yearly at the head of numberless fiestas and parades, the apotheosis of Anza, Moraga, Ortega, and Portolá.

Perhaps it is because they left no monuments except the land they found that these adventurers remain so shadowy in our minds. Later Californians—Spaniards, Russians, Mexicans, Yankees—built mission chapels and adobe barracks and sawmills that can be photographed and picnicked at. To find the ghosts of the conquistadores, one has to walk the windy ridges and the empty shores.

For the record, it was Ortega (Sergeant José) who, while scouting the peninsula in November 1769, in search of Monterey Bay (which the Spaniards had temporarily mislaid), stumbled upon the Golden Gate and thereby became the first white man (unless it was Drake) to see San Francisco Bay. It was Portolá (Captain Gaspar de), commander of the expedition, who had sent Ortega ahead and who, a few days later, climbed a ridge for a first view of the landlocked bay. It was the heroic Anza (Lieutenant Colonel Juan Bautista de) who led 240 colonists on an incredible thousand mile trek from Tubac, Arizona, to northern California in 1776 and selected spots where they would establish the Mission and Presidio of San Francisco; and it was Moraga (Lieutenant José Joaquin), Anza's able officer, who brought the settlers the last miles from Monterey to San Francisco.

Left: Gaspar de Portolá's first view of San Francisco Bay, painted with imaginative license by Walter Francis in 1909. Right: the same view today from a hill unromantically named Sweeney Ridge shows San Bruno and South San Francisco, in the middle distance, and Mount Diablo across the bay.

Costumed riders celebrated the two hundredth anniversary of Juan Bautista de Anza's trek by traveling in relays from Mexico City to San Francisco between September 1975 and March 1976, carrying Bicentennial flags, making speeches, and dedicating plaques.

Sand dunes at Fort Funston on the southwest edge of San Francisco are carpeted with native ice plants and sandhill daisies as they were when Portolá party rode up the coast, looking for Monterey. The distant headlands of Marin County, to the north, were Sergeant Ortega's destination on the day when he "discovered" an impassable gap in the shoreline, opening into a mighty bay.

Mission Dolores in 1830, as visualized fifty years later by artist Oriana Day, offered Mexican Californians such treats as a hanging-in-effigy of Judas Iscariot, celebrated with food and flirtation (above). By the 1890s the outbuildings had disappeared (below) and the mission was flanked by a fenced graveyard, a stuccoed parish house, and a brick Gothic church (leveled by the 1906 quake).

The Spanish Missionaries' Church of Sorrows

At last count there were 334,547 San Franciscans who never had seen and had no present intention of seeing the Mission of San Francisco de Asís, better known as Mission Dolores. Like the Statue of Liberty in New York, the mission is visited mainly by tourists and is regarded locally as Significant but Not Very Useful—an odd fate, indeed, for the only architectural relic of Spanish rule in San Francisco. Its history, a blank to most San Franciscans, has a certain mournful eloquence, for Dolores, like nearly all the California missions (and more so than many others,) was a death camp for its Indian converts. Along with Christian faith, Spanish language, and European agriculture, the missions brought cholera, measles, influenza, scabies, and venereal diseases. The Mission San Rafael, across the Golden Gate, was started as a sanitorium for the sick and dying of Dolores.

Juan Bautista de Anza, who led the city's first colonists from Mexico, chose the site by a marshy Lake (*Laguna de Manantial*) covering what is now roughly seventy blocks of the Mission District. Padre Francisco Palou celebrated Mass on the spot on June 29, 1776, and laid the cornerstone of the church six years later. The huge, imitation Spanish Baroque parish church next door, which lords it over the primitive colonial chapel, was built from 1913 to 1918. Because of its proximity to its humble neighbor, the new church has been a basilica since 1952.

A statue of Tekakwitha, "Lily of the Mohawks" (an Iroquois nation), is the only memorial to more than 5,500 Indians buried under mission grounds. The Franciscan system of conversion brought Indians into compounds, exposed them to European diseases, disrupted tribal methods of hygiene. The tragic result: almost total extermination of the people whom the missionaries came to "save."

The Farthest Outpost of a Doomed Empire

San Francisco began at the Presidio. In a sense, therefore, this 1,500-acre military reservation is the city's most historic spot, the physical remnant of a Spanish colonial enterprise that began in the year of the American Declaration of Independence.

But there is nothing Spanish nowadays about the Presidio except its name. Even the adobe hut that housed the Spanish *comandante* has been subsumed in a Yankee officers' mess with a red tile roof and vaguely Mexican décor.

The historic past that is clearly visible at the Presidio is that of the American 1870s, when the

post was headquarters for the Army's last campaign against the Modoc Indians, and of the 1880s, when various commanders occupied themselves between wars by having the barren slopes forested with cypress, pine, and eucalyptus trees.

Since the end of Spanish rule, the Presidio always has been comfortably behind the lines, a place of embarkation, occupation, and administration, never of siege and smoke. Most of the famous generals who have been posted here (William T. Sherman, Albert Sidney Johnston, Philip H. Sheridan, Hunter Liggett, Frederick Funston) came to the Presidio before or after the peak of their careers.

Perhaps that is why the historic pinnacle of the Presidio remains the moment of its founding on September 17, 1776, when, in the words of the Franciscan missionary Father Palou, "We took formal possession . . . in the name of our sovereign, with many discharges of cannon, both on sea and land, and the musketry of the soldiers." The rest has been two centuries of epilogue.

Far left: In the Presidio a light battery shows off cannon and horses outside red brick barracks in the 1870s. Above: The same barracks, still in use a century later, look calm and collegiate.

Lounging on barracks steps in the 1880s, soldiers pose (below left) with bayonets, pipes, and one billiard cue. Barracks life of the late 1970s (below right) includes a neatly uniformed woman a few feet from a sign warning: "No female guests permitted . . ."

Buried in the National Cemetery are Pauline Cushman Fryer, an actress who spied for the Union, and an Indian interpreter called "Two Bits."

Ceremonial occasions: On Independence Day, 1876 (far left), families in carriages watch a sham battle. On Memorial Day, 1975 (left), Sixth Army cannons fire a midday salute.

Portsmouth Square, 1879: Three decades of American rule already had erased every evidence that this once was the center of a Mexican village.

The First and Grabbed-off Square

There is ample testimony proving that Portsmouth Plaza used to be the town square of Yerba Buena before American troops arrived in 1846, hoisted their flag on the customhouse, and renamed the plaza to honor the ship that had brought them there.

A good thing it is, too, for of visible evidence there is none. Fires destroyed the Mexican buildings and the flimsy casinos that succeeded them, and the 1906 disaster effected another radical redevelopment. The ultimate metamorphosis was achieved by a series of city administrations that first dug a parking garage under the square, replaced the park above it with a chaotic roof garden, then authorized a footbridge over the whole mess to provide a grand concourse into a new hotel.

Outdoor games run all year, and picnics on what remains of the lawn are as pleasant as they were in the 1890s, when Chinese parents wore queues and children wore padded jackets.

Portsmouth Square, 1977: A century of further progress has now transformed the Yankee square into a giant knickknack shelf, with layers of cars underneath, card shelters and playgrounds on the terraces, and a pedestrian causeway overhead.

A Union Fortress Three Thousand Miles from War

If old Fort Point had not been blessed with a superb setting and an imposing, castle-like appearance, it undoubtedly would have been torn down years ago. In the whole crowded field of redundant military architecture, Fort Point is the ultimate embarrassment, having been both obsolete and useless from the day it was completed in 1861—a West Coast counterpart to vulnerable Fort Sumter in Charleston Harbor.

Fortunately, foolish heads prevailed, and the great brick bastion was not torn down—instead it has become a National Historic Monument. To this day, historians ponder whether any fortress was needed in far California to repel a Confederate invasion or any other sort of invasion; but there is no question that Fort Point would have been completely helpless if an enemy had appeared.

It makes a marvelous park—vast and spooky, like a gigantic red sand castle. There is a delightful irony, too, in its being preserved as a military museum: Fort Point would serve better as a national monument to military extravagance.

Squatting on a slab of rock at the south edge of the strait, Fort Point in the 1870s looked more imposing than the Spanish Castillo de San Joaquin, which originally had occupied the site. That fortress was so loosely held by Mexico in 1846 that John Charles Frémont was able to cross the strait one night by rowboat and spike the rusty cannon.

When the fort went into service in 1861, the seaside walls prickled with more than a hundred muzzle-loading, smooth-bore cannon. Within a year rifled guns made the battery technically obsolete.

Guns were manned at Fort Point through the turn of the century, and World War I trainees were quartered in the barracks. In World War II the Army used the building as a warehouse and corporation yard.

Overwhelmed by the Golden Gate Bridge, Fort Point now looks like a toy, although its walls of brick and granite are five to eight feet thick. Chief engineer Joseph Strauss had planned to anchor the bridge at the site of the fort but changed his design after touring the building.

Visitors to the Golden Gate National Recreation Area prowl the three-tiered battlements, listen to Civil War bugle calls, and perform gun drills under instruction of guides in the uniform of Union soldiers.

Miles of empty tunnels and gun galleries whistling in the wind impress visitors, who seldom suspect that this medieval ruin is better suited to entertaining visitors than it ever was to fortifying the coast.

On Nob Hill after the quake-fire catastrophe only two familiar shapes remained: silver millionaire James Flood's Connecticut brownstone mansion (now the Pacific Union Club) and the unfinished Fairmont Hotel, badly damaged but not destroyed. Among the missing was the Towne residence (center right), a restrained newcomer in a neighborhood of flamboyant Gothic castles. Designed by the city's foremost architect, Arthur Page Brown, and his ebullient assistant, Willis Polk, it had stood for almost two decades at the southwest corner of California and Taylor Streets, site today of the Masonic Auditorium. Weakened by the quake, the stately house burned as quickly as a South of Market tenement, leaving only its Ionic portico and brick façade, with a distinctive ogived window visible in the ruin (bottom right).

The Mournful Vestige of a Vanished Era

Six pillars of white marble, topped with a sculptured cornice, stand at the edge of a shadowy pond just north of the main drive in Golden Gate Park. They are all that remain of the Colonial Revival mansion of a railroad executive named A. N. Towne, which occupied a splendid corner on Nob Hill from the mid-1880s until April 18, 1906.

At 5 A.M. that day the earth beneath San Francisco, and for dozens of miles north and south, heaved and shuddered for almost a minute. Walls collapsed, pavements buckled, gas lines burst, water mains went dry—and for seventy-two hours the city burned.

It was neither the first nor the last major earthquake to strike the Bay Area. A powerful tremor, centered down the Peninsula, had been recorded in 1838. There were nasty little shakes in 1864, a whopper in 1865, and another in 1868, known for almost forty years as "The Great Earthquake."

In a sense the Portals of the Past are a monument to everything San Francisco lost in the 1906 disaster—512 blocks demolished, $500 million in property destroyed, 250,000 homeless, 700 dead or missing—and to the "glad, mad spirit," as Gelett Burgess called it, of the city that was.

The temple-like portico, rescued by a group headed by U. S. Senator James Phelan, a onetime mayor of the city, stands now in a grove of eucalyptus, pines, and Irish yew. In 1957 one of the inner columns crumbled (left), felled by an earthquake.

EXPRESS

A Survivor of the Crucible

When word got around in the late 1960s that the federal government wanted to sell the "old" San Francisco Mint to land developers, elder citizens laughed and shook their heads.

"Tear down the Mint? Why, that building survived the Earthquake! You'd pay more to knock it down than the land is worth."

It was back in 1870 that the Treasury Department, weary of its cramped, acid-stained branch mint on Commercial Street, had ordered a magnificent new edifice in the Greek Revival style of the period. The walls were of brick, three feet thick, faced with a foot of granite at the base and with sandstone on the upper stories—a noble temple to the majesty of American mazuma. It became for a time the largest manufactory of coins in the world, serving foreign governments as well as that of the United States, stamping out millions of five-dollar gold pieces, ten-dollar eagles, twenty-dollar double eagles, and two (2) three-dollar gold pieces, now worth at least fifty thousand each. Water cisterns in the inner court saved the building from the fires of 1906, and it functioned as a reserve bank and depository for the shattered city.

In 1937 the branch moved its operations again, up Market Street to a marble fortress on a knob of rock. For thirty years the abandoned temple harbored little orphan agencies, put there by General Services. Mayors and college presidents and real estate brokers hankered for the site. The preservers won in 1972, when President Nixon signed an order returning the Old Mint, now a National Historic Building, to the Treasury with instructions to convert it to a museum of coinage and Far Western history and a mail-order center for distributing special coins and medals.

A century of use, abuse, and near-disaster is eclipsed in two views of the Mint at Fifth and Mission Streets. The building's mint condition speaks well for Federal-Greek-Revival architecture, but also reflects recent replacement of crumbling cornices and guano-splattered pediments with new trimmings of fake stone and fiber glass.

A nineteenth-century coin stamp that punched out Double Eagles in the 1850s (top) still rolls out coins in demonstrations at the Old Mint Museum.

In the Mint's adjusting room in the 1870s employees weighed gold blanks before sending them to the stamper. Women wore linen aprons, oversleeves, and gloves while filing down overweight coins, and all garments were brushed before the worker left the room. The Mint was fussy about leakage.

A Victorian Fantasy of Flowers Under Glass

James Lick, who made a fortune in San Francisco real estate, died before he could enjoy the fancy greenhouse he had ordered from England to ornament the garden of his home in the Santa Clara Valley. Like the rest of Lick's $3 million estate, the conservatory, a replica of one in Kew Gardens, London, went to a worthy charity—in this case, the people of San Francisco, who set up the many-faceted glass jewel on a knoll in Golden Gate Park in 1879 and have been admiring it ever since.

Margot Patterson Doss, the city's indefatigable walking guide, observed that the conservatory looked "as though it had been contrived overnight of gossamer and the wings of moths." In fact, construction took three years and cost forty thousand dollars. Over the years, the conservatory has been partially destroyed by fire (1882), several times enlarged, and repeatedly vandalized. It is, withal, considerably sturdier than it looks—a comforting condition for the most outrageous, anachronistic, and adorable of municipal souvenirs.

Backdrop of innumerable photographs, the conservatory and its doormat of floral parquetry welcomed the Grand Army of the Republic to San Francisco in 1903, when the above picture was taken. In 1976, when park gardeners posed in the same setting, the flowers greeted school volunteers.

A visit to the conservatory to see the eighteen-inch blossoms and six-foot leaf pads of a giant water lily was regarded circa 1880 as a zesty date. The Victoria regia lily, named for the Queen of England, came from London, which may have accounted for its chic. Nowadays, visitors flock in for seasonal shows of cyclamens, tuberous begonias, and other tender plants.

IRRIGATED
COME
LAND
M. A. GUNST & CO.

Lotta's Little Legacy and How It Grew

It was a gift to dogs and horses, and for more than a century scarcely anyone has looked it in the mouth. Critics have had their say, of course, comparing it to a Bavarian bedpost or a fancy stovepipe in the parlor of a Comstock millionaire. And it has been assaulted by earthquakes and vandals, wayward cars and willful remodelers.

Charlotte Mignon (Lotta) Crabtree, the brashest, bounciest entertainer of her day, gave the fountain to the city to thank the local admirers who had launched her career as a squirmy tease of eight in 1854. Lotta, with characteristic gusto, thought up the design herself, basing it on a lighthouse in one of the sixty farces with which she enraptured the music halls of America. San Francisco, with characteristic insouciance, erected it on what was and remains one of the busiest downtown intersections, at Market, Kearny, and Geary Streets.

Lotta's Fountain circa 1905 (left) was an awkward twenty-four-foot stump, topped with gas lamps and iron filigree, but it served admirably as a watering trough, rendezvous, and traffic hazard. The generous donor posed for the demure photograph below at the height of her fame in the 1870s. On stage, Lotta dressed up in burned cork, fright wigs, and baggy trousers, danced hornpipes and Irish jigs, and bellowed out a leather-lunged parody of Jenny Lind.

Shifted a few feet southeast in 1974, the fountain now squats on a triangular traffic island. In 1916 city engineers added eight feet to the column to raise the lamp to the level of new lights on Market Street. Lotta's gift cost $8,475, including freight, from a Philadelphia foundry. Sentimental San Franciscans have spent a hundred times that in maintenance, repairs, and remodeling.

"The Palace shows the mortality of grandeur and the vanity of human wishes," Bernard Maybeck said of his gloomy masterpiece. Inspired by Piranesi's drawings of Roman ruins, the domed rotunda and curving peristyle of Corinthian columns showed carefully contrived decay even when brand new.

A Haunting Souvenir of an Innocent Affair

A decade of creativity, sacrifice, and missed opportunities following the earthquake-fire culminated in 1915 with the Panama-Pacific International Exposition, a $50 million efflorescence of Beaux-Arts architecture, kitsch paintings, stunt fliers, visiting statesmen, dance pavilions, and junk food, celebrating both the completion of the interocean canal and the rebuilding of San Francisco.

The theme building was the Tower of Jewels, seven stories of plaster wedding cake emblazoned with fifty thousand gems of glass that trembled and sparkled by night in the gleam of searchlights. But it was Bernard Maybeck's Palace of Fine Arts, crumbling by a dark lagoon, that became the beloved and only memento of the fair. Reconstructed in the 1960s by private citizens and public agencies

The Tower of Jewels is near center, the rotunda of the Palace at far right in this panorama of the 1915 exposition. To create space for the fair, the city filled more than 180 acres of tidal swamp once known inelegantly as Washerwoman's Lagoon. After the exposition the area became the Marina District and its esplanade.

A Carter-Ford debate attracted several thousand noisy friends of African independence, abortion, disarmament, anarchy, fetal rights, pay increases for federal workers, socialism, Nazism, women's rights, and whales. The Palace is a cynosure to duck-feeders, swan-lovers, and television film crews. (Cops and robbers love terra cotta columns.)

($2 million each from the city, the state, and philanthropist Walter S. Johnson), the Palace floats like a huge, reddish-gold bubble among the low, graveled roofs of the Marina District. Its barny galleries now house a splendid museum of science and a theater that has accommodated auctions, concerts, film festivals, and a 1976 presidential campaign debate between Gerald Ford and Jimmy Carter.

Exploratorium, an imaginative museum of science conceived and directed by Dr. Frank Oppenheimer, has filled the cavernous shell of the rebuilt art gallery with more than two hundred exhibits in which visitors test their perceptions of light and color, space and sound. Musical instruments "play" colors, furniture vibrates under the impact of cosmic rays, and explorers wallow, crawl, and slither in total darkness, guided by only the sense of touch, through a multichambered "Tactile Gallery" inside a geodesic dome.

Rumbling gently through the Western Addition, a ninety-year-old Victorian row house begins a new life in a renewal area ten blocks from its original site. Like the Italianate house (right), it will get new plumbing, wiring, and bright paint inside and out.

CHAPTER 7

Transformations, Saves, and Total Losses

Let us now mourn famous buildings.

Gone forever is the Parrott Block, first masonry office tower (three stories) in Western America, built of granite cubes precut in China and assembled on the northwest corner of California and Montgomery Streets in 1852 by a crew from Canton. Like a testament from the past, enduring fire and earthquake, it stood until 1926, when it was torn down to be replaced by the Financial Center Building. . . .

Gone, long gone, the low-slung adobe customhouse, seat of power and rectitude in the Mexican pueblo of Yerba Buena and location of the roof beam where the Vigilantes elongated the neck of John Jenkins in the spring of 1851, a few months before the building (along with most of the rest of the town) disappeared in flames. . . .

Gone the Humphreys House (1852), with cupola and picket fence, which held its ground at the crest of Hyde and Chestnut Streets for almost a century, escaping destruction in 1906 through the timely aid of a west wind, a garden cistern, and a company of volunteers well moistened with Roederer champagne—only to succumb quietly in 1947 to the wrecking ball of an apartment house builder. . . .

Gone the Sweeney Observatory, a *fin-de-siècle* Far Western Stonehenge, perched on the crown of four-hundred foot Strawberry Hill in Golden Gate Park, whence it afforded a romantic vista from sea to bay for innumerable Sunday carriage parties until it crumbled into reddish rubble with the first temblor of April 18, 1906. . . .

Gone the 4,652-seat Fox, the ultimate motion picture palace of the Pacific Coast, the Moorish jewel of upper Market Street, sold for scrap after the city's voters in 1961 turned down a proposal to buy it for $1,150,000, a tiny fraction of its present replacement value. . . .

Gone the Montgomery Block, the Allyne House, Fort Gunnybags, Maguire's Opera House . . . gone Sutro Baths, Tait's-at-the-Beach, the Alcazar. . . .

In haste—and with no little awe—let us praise the saved, the loved, the usefully transformed.

Saved the Abner Phelps house, the oldest unchanged residence in the city, hidden inside a block west of Divisadero Street between Oak and Page, just where the young lawyer had it built in 1850 of materials brought around the Horn from New Orleans. . . .

Saved the Audiffred Building (1889), an oddly mansarded brick structure on Mission Street at the Embarcadero that looks like a sailors' hotel on the waterfront in Le Havre—which is undoubtedly what the French builder, Hippolyte d'Audiffred, intended. . . .

Saved St. Patrick's Church, on Mission Street near Third, which once called itself "The Most Irish Church in America" and, having wound up on skid row, became the only building with any distinction in an area marked for urban renewal. . . .

Saved James Flood's Connecticut brownstone mansion on Nob Hill, an appropriately regal headquarters for the exclusive Pacific Union Club. . . .

Saved the Garden Court of the Palace Hotel, the Old Transamerica Building, the South San Francisco Opera House, the Columbus Tower, the firehouse of Engine Company No. 22, the Belli Building, the San Francisco Gas Company (Merryvale), One Jackson Place, the Hallidie Building. . . .

Do the saves outweigh the losses? Do the useful transformations mitigate the reckless waste? A pessimist would say that what remains is a small fragment of lost heritage. The optimists, bless them, are busy converting foundries into boutiques and circulating petitions to save the neighborhood hardware store from becoming a savings and loan.

Stricken with technological obsolescence, Stanford University's 1893 Lane Hospital capitulates to radical surgery in 1974. A decade earlier Stanford moved its medical school to Palo Alto, selling its city properties to the Presbyterian Hospital of Pacific Medical Center.

False-front façades on Montgomery Street north of Washington looked like a set for a Western movie a month after the 1906 catastrophe (above), but several have outlived more pretentious buildings. Three at mid-block, built in 1851, are now designated historic landmarks. They house decorators' showrooms, studios, and the offices of trial lawyer Melvin Belli.

The Sparing of the Square

Inexplicably, the blow that struck the city in '06 glanced off some of its oldest buildings—loft factories, printshops, whorehouses, and other antiques along what used to be the shore of the bay.

Even then, three quarters of a century ago, it was a faded neighborhood from which the fancy haberdasheries and theaters of the '50s and '60s had departed to newer business districts. Cigarmakers, liquor dealers, and impoverished artists occupied the sturdy little brick boxes on Montgomery and Jackson Streets and Jones Alley, and they alone rejoiced when fortune spared this humble territory from destruction. Not only did a noted distillery escape Jehovah's wrath, most of its neighbors also shared in the passover. Many of these relics were still around, shabby but charming in their dotage, when changing tastes and rising real estate values brought a group of furniture and fabric wholesalers into the 400 block of Jackson Street in the early 1950s.

Sandblasted and gilded, adorned with lamps and laurel trees, the neglected block became Jackson Square, a model of sensible architectural restoration. Jones Alley was reincarnated into Hotaling Place. Twenty years later, the city established its first historic preservation district in the six surrounding blocks, thereby providing a tardy answer to Charles K. Field's frequently quoted jingle (1906):

> If, as they say, God spanked the town
> for being over-frisky,
> Why did He burn the churches down
> and spare Hotaling's Whisky?

Hotaling's warehouse, built in 1866, having celebrated its divine salvation by resuming shipments of Old Kirk Whisky a few weeks after the earthquake-fire, succumbed to the double damper of Prohibition and Depression in the 1930s (above). Refurbished and repainted, it is now a showroom for whosesale furnishings.

The action on Jackson, always fashionable and often fetching, commands the attention of a second-story spectator on a fall afternoon in the late 1970s. Although the entire neighborhood is dedicated to historic preservation, its businesses and customers are ardently stylish.

The Uncanny Metamorphosis of a Packing Plant

From time to time somebody comes up with a really terrible idea like, "Why don't we turn an out-of-date fruit cannery into a sort of shopping and browsing place, with trees and views and music?" and all over town people shake their heads and smile in anticipation of the coming disaster.

The Cannery, having completed sixty years or so of homely service to the food processing industry, was awaiting the wrecker's ball in the early 1960s when the terrible idea struck an investor-developer named Leonard V. Martin. Impressed by the transformation of the nearby Ghirardelli chocolate factory into a sparkling shopping center, Martin hired three imaginative advisers (Joseph Esherick, architect; Thomas D. Church, landscape architect; and Marget Larsen, designer), rounded up $8 million, and proceeded to demonstrate that all it takes are brains, taste, energy, and money to turn a really terrible idea into a vast success.

Amazing how an old factory is enhanced by the addition of a grove of olive trees, a well-stocked gourmet food shop, several outstanding restaurants, a splendid bookstore, a cinema, a terrace cafe—and who said it was a terrible idea?

The Cannery in 1905 was a lumpish block of dark red brick on a waterfront strewn with rubble and smoldering trash. Initials on the building stood for California Fruit Canners Association, which in 1916 joined three other West Coast food processors to form California Packing Corporation, now the multinational San Francisco-based Del Monte Corporation, an R. J. Reynolds subsidiary.

Old-fashioned but turning out tons of tinned vegies every year, the cannery provided welcome jobs for families in surrounding North Beach in the lean years of the '30s.

The courtyard of The Cannery was once a railroad siding, and now offers shaded picnic tables and free concerts. The arched doors and windows, raised cornices, and protruding masonry bolts are architectural features preserved from the old warehouse west of the main factory.

The Born-Again Victorians

It was roughly fifteen years ago, while public and private redevelopers were competing to see who would knock down the largest number of nineteenth-century houses, that the cult of Victorian preservation suddenly swept over San Francisco with the force of a new state religion.

For decades persons of small means and elaborate taste had been quietly evangelizing on behalf of so-called monstrosities of Carpenter Gothic. Now, in joyful conversion, thousands of others discovered the unique local architecture: narrow row houses, built of thousand-year-old virgin redwood, decorated with outlandish wooden scrollwork, and blessed with soaring ceilings and tall bay windows to catch every ray of sunshine in a chill, seaside climate.

What an outburst there was of newspaper articles, books, walking tours, slide shows, and federal grants exploring the nuances of Italianate, Eastlake, Stick-style, and Queen Anne! What a flowering of purple pediments and gilded gables on the grimy gray façades of the inner Mission District, the Haight-Ashbury, and the Western Addition!

Indeed, gentle reader, there were persons within the Movement who vouchsafed it had gone entirely too far, confusing ugliness with charm and painting every bit of trim a different shade of plum, and it was high time we rediscovered the classic lines and hidden value of the Sunset District Junior Five.

An Italianate residence at 1707 Broderick Street in San Francisco's Western Addition weathered almost a century of occupancy since its construction in the 1880s (upper left), undergoing several metamorphoses along the way. In 1940 (center), in accord with prevailing distaste for gingerbread, its owners had the house stripped of ornamental eaves, scroll-sawn window frames, and neoclassic balusters and given a tidy shell of low-maintenance asbestos shingles. Thousands of nineteenth-century houses (those that were not torn down) endured similar plastic surgery, which was thought at the time to be the only sensible way to deal with Victorian excrescences. In 1975 (upper right), with excrescences back in vogue, contractors specializing in restoration peeled off the siding, recreated the original redwood millwork, and gave the house a coat of blue with white trim to show off its eccentricities. A modern touch remains: the one-car garage tucked under the bow window of the parlor.

The Cadoza residence on Haight Street near Divisadero, resplendent with Corinthian columns and Baroque entablature when it was new in the 1890s (far left), is now a three-unit apartment, hiding most of its Victorian origins (though not its side wall) under a mask of tan stucco and a dizzy little beret of Spanish tiles.

SKATE

Fun House, with whirling floors, trick mirrors, and skirt-lifting air jets, outlived other concessions into the 1960s. In the '40s (above) it was a social nucleus for sailors on liberty and high school girls in bobby socks who would top off the evening with an enchilada and an "It's It" ice cream sandwich.

Playland Remembered

There is no place in San Francisco any more like Playland-at-the-Beach, a weather-beaten luna park that some people thought was thrilling, others thought was vulgar, and fewer and fewer thought was amusing.

Playland opened in the 1890s, when Ferris wheels and merry-go-rounds were the ultimate carnival rides and nobody had heard of Disney or Marriott. At best it was an undersized provincial cousin of Coney Island, but it enchanted generations of young San Franciscans and made a fortune for the brothers George and Leo Whitney, who owned and ran it from the 1920s until it was overwhelmed in the 1960s by the seductive rivalry of television and of "theme parks" populated with electrified rhinoceri and singing dolls.

When feather boas were in vogue, an ostrich farm had occupied the site. Lately, an entrepreneur has been talking of filling it with apartments. To those who remember, it will always be the-place-where-Playland-was—redolent of fried onions, armpits, and caramel corn, resounding eternally to the recorded laughter of the Fun House, the crack of rifles, and the shrieks of roller coaster riders plunging earthward through the fog.

Playland drew thousands to the beach on sunny weekends in the 1940s (top). In the late '70s only rubble, sand, and a chain-link fence remained.

The Montgomery Block in 1856 (above) and its replacement in 1976 (below). Transamerica's inventive public relations persons, sensing San Francisco's weakness for impudence, call this spike "The Pyramid . . . a San Francisco landmark since 1972." When like our sires our sons are gone, the resentment will perhaps be forgotten, the outrage forgiven, and the slogan accepted as evidence of corporate wit.

A Missing Link

For as long as it stood—and it did so for more than a hundred years—a weary, grayish-brown office building at the southeast corner of Washington and Montgomery Streets was one of the esteemed edifices of the West, one that, had it survived even ten years longer, undoubtedly would have appeared in the chapter on cherished relics, rather than here among the irretrievable losses.

The Montgomery Block, known in its dotage as the Monkey Block, was the first substantial commercial structure in western America. Henry W. Halleck, a young lawyer who was later to become general-in-chief of the Union armies, raised the prodigious sum of $3 million to construct the four-story colossus on a giant raft of logs and pilings and bay mud in 1853. For decades, its size, its fireproof walls, its distinguished occupants, its palm-bowered lobby, and its celebrated Bank Exchange saloon made it the city's business and intellectual center.

Longevity, alone, should have marked the Monkey Block for protection as the most important link between the modern city and the gold rush, but the Block also developed rich associations with generations of artists, writers, saints, and madmen who tenanted its low-rent rooms when decay set in—Ambrose Bierce, Maynard Dixon, George Sterling, Gelett Burgess, Homer Lea, Sun Yat-sen.

Enough. In 1959 a wizard who had learned that parking lots were more profitable than buildings ordered the Monkey Block torn down, the site paved, and an attendant in a white smock installed to collect charges. To complete the improvements, the Transamerica Corporation, a diverse financial institution whose original purposes have been forgotten, built there a tower of odd design, by no accident the tallest west of the Mississippi.

Outside the Bank Exchange in 1856 an editor named James Casey shot an editor named James King, who called himself "of William" in distinction from others of the name. When King died in the Montgomery Block a few days later, the Vigilantes hanged Casey and another handy prisoner, Charles Cora, thereby enhancing the city's repute as a place of firm, if not necessarily legal, discipline. The Bank Exchange, re-established on the ground floor of the Transamerica Building, displays historical artifacts and serves what is said to be an authenic, re-creation of the bar's famous Pisco Punch.

First City Hall (above), at the northwest corner of Kearny and Pacific, was destroyed by fire in 1851. No. 2 (right), on Kearny near Washington, was remodeled from a theater and two saloons, lasted until 1895.

If You Can't Beat It . . .

Back when San Francisco consisted of a mission, a barracks, and some cattle sheds, the alcalde held court and signed land grants in an adobe shanty on the town square. It was a state of affairs that no Yankee town could tolerate. In 1850, City Hall, the central nervous system of American civic life, came to California in the form of a three-story mansion, prefabricated in Baltimore and shipped around the Horn.

Burned out a year later, the city fathers sought

No. 3 opened at Larkin and Grove in 1897. This basilica took twenty-seven years to build and collapsed in forty-eight seconds in the 1906 earthquake. Reformers saw it as a symbol of the quality of local government in the age of gold and silver.

The temporary City Hall (from 1907 to 1916) was a hotel at Tenth and Market. Drafted into municipal service after the earthquake-fire, it later reverted to the Whitcomb, is now the San Franciscan Hotel.

Move It

shelter in a theater that happened to belong to a close friend of the local Democratic boss. So it went, like the chambered nautilus, until the joyful day in 1916 when the Mayor of San Francisco was able to boast that the dome of the newest City Hall on Van Ness Avenue was (as it still is) sixteen feet taller than that of the national capitol. God willing, the cycle of growth is complete, and the shell, not yet outworn, will cradle the restless nautilus for generations to come.

The Renaissance dome of the present City Hall, dedicated in late 1915, is a landmark and a target of abuse. Above: a welcome to men of the American Expeditionary Force returning from Europe in 1919. Below: the noontime scene in the late 1970s—strollers, sheet-metal sculptures, and guerrilla theater on an obscurely unpatriotic theme.

Apartments and an entrance to Civic Center BART station fill the gap in the block, but not in the Swiss-cheese-and-Greek-olive trade.

The Ultimate Mama-and-Papa Store

It is highly unlikely that any historical society will affix a bronze marker on the site of the Crystal Palace Market at Eighth and Market Streets. A commercial establishment of middle age and undistinguished aspect, it succumbed in August 1959 to prolonged economic illness complicated by a changing population. Its closing left an emptiness in the hearts of a generation of San Franciscans who loved to wander the narrow aisles, breathing the mingled essences of ripe cheese, dill pickles, and

fresh coffee, buying sacks of chestnuts, slices of mortadella, bottles of herb vinegar, and bowls of fresh fruit with yogurt.

The Crystal Palace left no heirs, unless one counts the Marina Safeway. There, even the meats are wrapped in plastic packages and the only fragrance is of Yves St. Laurent cologne on customers shopping one another among the frozen pizzas. Where the Crystal stood there is now a failed commercial hotel, converted into apartments and offices. Gone are the gunny-bags of lentils, the barrels of shriveled olives, the mountains of garlic, the greetings shouted back and forth in Italian or Serbo-Croat—gone all traces of the last of the multi-concession downtown markets.

A health food counter, festooned with real tinsel for Christmas, 1953, dished up gallons of yogurt to patrons who attributed medicinal, if not supernatural, powers to Bulgarian cultured milk. No one thought of freezing *it. Below: A normal day of temptation and indecision at the cheese stand and an extraordinary day of bargains at the meat market before the doors closed forever.*

NATIONAL MARITIME MUSEUM AT SAN FRANCISCO

Balclutha, *as she was in the late 1880s, with topsails furled to the yardarms and decks awash, bucks heavy seas on one of her seventeen voyages around the Horn. The painting was done by Oswald Brett in 1955, the year of* Balclutha*'s restoration as an exhibit ship.*

Last of the Cape Horn Fleet

Built and launched in Glasgow, Scotland, in 1886, the square-rigged sailing vessel *Balclutha* was a typical British merchant ship of the late nineteenth century. For thirteen years she sailed in the deep-water trade, one of hundreds of cargo ships that would round Cape Horn each year to load California grain for Europe, returning with hardware from Belgium, liquors from England, coal from Wales.

But for more than thirty years—first as a lumber ship, then in the Alaskan salmon trade—she called San Francisco her home port, and it is here that she has come to rest as a museum ship. Dozens of donors contributed funds in 1953 to snatch *Balclutha* from the hammers and torches of scrap dealers. Corraled (and often goaded) by Karl Kortum, director of the San Francisco Maritime Museum, labor unions and individuals volunteered thirteen thousand hours of work, and more than ninety business firms contributed $100,000 in supplies to an authentic and loving restoration of the lone relic of the Cape Horn trade on the Pacific Coast.

NATIONAL MARITIME MUSEUM AT SAN FRANCISCO

Helmsman eyes the skysails as Balclutha*—then known as* Star of Alaska*—gets underway on a long trip north in 1925. Under charter to the Alaska Packers Association, she carried workers and supplies to canneries on Kodiak Island, brought back thousands of cases of canned salmon.*

Wandering on decks and in cargo holds, visitors today recapture the decades when Balclutha *plied the oceans of the world, loading rice in Rangoon, nitrate in Chile, guano in Callao, wool in New Zealand. Admission charges pay for operation and maintenance of the ship and help support the nonprofit Maritime Museum.*

Young crewman takes the helm on a voyage of the imagination from Balclutha's *permanent berth at Pier 43, near Fisherman's Wharf. Underway, the ship would carry a crew of twenty-six men.*

Two of Eight

At one time, according to a local guidebook-writing tradition, there were eight octagonal houses in San Francisco. The number is unconvincingly pat, like seven or forty in an Arabian tale, but the total has been eroded to only two: a strangely haunting house at 1067 Green Street, on Russian Hill, and a misplaced specimen of New England-Greek Revival domestic architecture at 2645 Gough Street. They are among the few remainders, anywhere, of a mid-nineteenth-century architectural cult that inflamed its followers with the sort of fanaticism associated nowadays with geodesic domes, pyramids, and solar panels. The high priest was a genius named Orson S. Fowler, a practitioner of hydrotherapy and phrenology as well as architecture, whose book *A Home for All* promised not only cheap housing (a family could build an octagon for a hundred dollars, he said) but also robust health due to the salubrious influence of cement-and-gravel walls and windows boxing the compass. A further asset, which Fowler probably did not foresee, was durability. Neither beauty nor historical associations could so effectively have protected the octagons from destruction as their single unique attribute—their odd shape.

This Neo-Colonial octagon, on the west side of Gough Street near Union, was constructed in the early 1860s on the opposite side of the street by William C. McElroy, a mill operator. Moved and restored in 1952 by the National Society of Colonial Dames, it is the organization's Western headquarters and museum. Under the clapboard siding—which is merely decoration—are the walls of lime and gravel prescribed by Orson Fowler.

When the 1906 earthquake tumbled one wall of the Gough Street octagon (left) the resident Cavagnaro family lost confidence in the remaining seven and decamped. The Green Street octagon (below) was built about 1855 by a French immigrant named Feusier, whose family occupied the house for eighty-five years. The recent photograph at right shows a mansard roof and more dormer windows added in the 1880s.

St. Mary's— Old, New, Newest

Three cathedral churches, each dedicated to the Virgin Mary, have served as the seat of the Roman Catholic Archbishop of San Francisco since the city's first prelate, the Most Reverend Sadoc Alemany, consecrated the simple, red brick church now known as Old St. Mary's on Christmas Eve, 1854.

The first, built of bricks brought around the Horn from New England and granite cut in China, survived the disaster of 1906 and another blaze that charred the interior in 1966. The second St. Mary's (1891–1962) was burned beyond repair. A television station occupies its former site. The third, called by some critics the most beautiful and by others the most banal of modern ecclesiastical buildings, dominates a redeveloped neighborhood that has taken the name Cathedral Hill. Outspoken newspaper columnists and Catholic laymen argued that $7 million to build an edifice might better be spent on human needs, but there is no question that the new St. Mary's, like it or not, is the most distinctive landmark of its name to grace the Archdiocese of San Francisco.

Old St. Mary's towered over low buildings at California and Dupont (now Grant Avenue) in the 1870s. Dedicated in 1854, it served as a cathedral for nearly four decades; it is now a Paulist mission to Chinatown.

St. Mary's II on Van Ness at O'Farrell witnessed innumerable ordinations, celebrations, and civic funerals from 1891 to 1962. Over the years, the once-fashionable residential district became the city's Automobile Row.

New St. Mary's, rimmed by mosaic esplanades and landscaped parking lots, occupies two city blocks at Geary and Gough, seats 2,400 with standing room for 2,000 more. The 189-foot cupola rests on a huge pylon at each of its corners.

Raging fire on a Friday night in September 1962 destroyed the Van Ness Avenue cathedral. Although few admired its Late Union Depot façade, designed by Chicago architects, many mourned the loss of a familiar institution.

Archbishop Joseph T. McGucken posed in the ruins to launch a drive for new St. Mary's. Some liberals called the project "vain" and "wasteful"; radicals threatened to bomb the building; but most Catholics approved of the structure, fondly dubbed "McGucken's Maytag."

The German Gothic interior of the old cathedral (below left) and the soaring hollow shell of the new (below right) reflect change of doctrine as well as taste. Pews form a U around the predella, and no member of the congregation is more than seventy-five feet back. The glittering baldachin above the altar is made of thousands of thin aluminum rods.

After the earthquake, shock left many survivors catatonic, like this woman who sits numbly among trunks and a treadle sewing machine, while others pick through the ruins of a house.

The Agonizing Loss, the Incredible Rebirth

The disaster of April 1906 proved that transformations, saves, and total losses all may be accomplished more or less simultaneously by the same agency within a few days' time.

No one was completely satisfied with the results.

Why (a local poet asked) did God knock the churches down and spare Hotaling's Whisky? Why did the Hall of Records, with its unique municipal documents, perish in flaming rubble? Why did the awkward Call Building survive to become the prosaic Central Tower? Why was the city rebuilt precisely as it was before, ignoring the imaginative alternatives presented by Daniel H. Burnham, the dean of American city planners?

Reflecting on the toll of that calamity (which has since been exceeded in so many other cities), one cannot evaluate the gains and losses. It is possible only to say that the evil was sufficient unto the day, and to pray that so great a transformation, so vast a loss, never shall visit us again.

Nob Hill in late April 1906 (left), with the blackened remains of Chinatown in the foreground and the shell of the Fairmont Hotel at the crest. The same vista in 1977 (above) is largely blocked by buildings, but the Fairmont is still visible, just to the right of its flag-topped annex, a tower much taller than itself.

Cottages for the homeless filled the empty dunes of the Richmond District along what is now Park-Presidio Boulevard (right). Although this ephemeral community disappeared a few years after the quake, a few earthquake cottages remain, including one behind the two-story white building (upper right) at Clement and Funston Streets.

A full-dress outing in the early 1870s (top) brought a harem-like group to the lawns of Golden Gate Park, then only two or three years old. More than a century later, the park still invites family outings and youthful exuberance (above and right).

CHAPTER 8

Out in the Cool Pacific Breeze

Unlike the chesty, barefoot towns of Southern California, San Francisco has never bragged much about its climate. In truth, the San Francisco climate is nothing to brag about: a desert rainfall (twenty-one inches,) concentrated from November through March; an arid spring; a chilling summer of gray flannel fogs; a blazing autumn of hot flashes, muted trees, and pungent yellow haze above the flatlands of the bay. The first Americans in Yerba Buena thought it must be the most repulsive place on earth—howling winds, swirling sand, and leaden skies in August.

Yet the San Francisco climate has always had admirers. You see them outdoors every day of the year, grateful to find the weather, as usual, monotonous but moderate, brisk but mild. The San Franciscan goes without an overcoat year round, picnics on the Marina Green in February, and takes his shirt off playing tennis in the park on New Year's Day. In midsummer, when air conditioners are groaning in Fresno and mothers in Los Angeles are calling their children inside to escape the smog, brokers on Montgomery Street are walking to lunch in the worsted suits they wore in January. Although there are few spectators who find night baseball in San Francisco an undiluted pleasure, no one, as far as we know, ever has frozen his nose at a football game.

Densely populated as the city is, its people always have rushed to outdoor pleasures. A visitor in the early 1880s discovered what may be the secret reason: "The air is tonic," he wrote, "touching every cheek with rosiest health and developing women into beings of transporting beauty . . ." A more than adequate compensation for enduring a spanking breeze, the gentleman said.

Two Pleasure Gardens in Their Time

When Robert B. Woodward, the culturally vulturous proprietor of the What Cheer House temperance hotel, decided in 1866 to open his private flower beds, art gallery, and animal wallow to his fellow-citizens at two bits a head, he provided San Francisco with its first family playground that was not also a beer hall, sand dune, or cemetery. A similar urge for civic betterment animated the latter-day millionaire William Matson Roth a century later to turn an outmoded chocolate factory into an inviting cluster of shops and restaurants called Ghirardelli Square.

There is more than a superficial resemblance between the two commercial parks. Woodward's, which occupied a four-acre block at Fourteenth and Mission Streets into the early 1890s, was a random gathering of enticements: stuffed monkeys, acrobats, boxing matches, theatricals, a tank of sea lions, a deer park, a Chinese giant, Roman chariot races, rifle drills, sword swallowers, balloon ascensions. By contrast, Ghirardelli Square, on a terraced slope overlooking the bay, is merely a pleasant shopping center of novel design. Its entertainments are sporadic (strolling musicians, Christmas tree lighting, flower shows); its restaurants, exotic (Hungarian, early Californian, North Chinese); its shops, rarefied (music boxes, Finnish jewelry, wine-making equipment, Turkish pastries, giant photographs).

The likeness is a matter of scale—of smallness without confinement, variety without excess. To most shoppers and strollers, Ghirardelli imparts a sense of leisure well spent, discovery shared, and intimacy enjoyed. That must have been some of the charm of Woodward's Gardens a hundred years ago.

Stuffed birds amused the kids at Woodward's Gardens in the 1880s. At Ghirardelli Square children fish for coins that visitors have thrown into Ruth Asawa's Mermaid Fountain. The stuffed fowl at right is a casual drop-in, not an inhabitant.

The gazebo on the Italian terrace of Woodward's Gardens (above) was a belvedere from which to admire the Mission District. The glassed octagon at Ghirardelli is a restaurant.

The red brick clock tower at North Point and Larkin Streets, symbol of Ghirardelli Square, was patterned on the château of Blois, France. Woodward's gate was a Renaissance arch surmounted by wooden statues of Queen Califa, the state's founding Amazon, and grizzly bears, our most impressive beast.

The Eternal Allure of Surf and Sky

Only a San Franciscan could love Ocean Beach, and even among San Franciscans this emotion is rare. The wild west wind comes romping in, the surf is cold, the undertow is fatally dangerous. It is no Copacabana.

A century ago the beach was a favorite race-course for young blades with rented carriages from the livery stables of Folsom Street. In a sense, it serves the same use today. Bikers and joggers trail along the hard sand, scattering the gulls; caballeros from stables in Golden Gate Park gallop on the bridle path that follows the crests of the dunes; and hot-rod drivers gather in the predawn hours for clandestine drag races on Great Highway, a two-hundred-foot-wide boulevard that was built atop a concrete seawall in the late 1920s to keep the sand ON the beach and OUT OF the park.

Only a few years ago, Great Highway was closed for almost two weeks by wind-driven sand—a fair display of the temperament of Ocean Beach.

An ambiguously smiling young woman of the Gibson Girl era shows the usual reaction of first-time visitors to Ocean Beach: disappointment, horror, and aching arches. Inveterate beach-goers, like the shepherd exercising his human on an afternoon in the 1970s, strip down to their own fur in every sort of weather and ignore the distraction of erotic sand sculptures.

Horseless carriages mingle with two-wheeled flies and equestrians in a charming jam-up of Sunday traffic on Great Highway around 1905 (top left). The vehicular parade now runs to sports cars, motor bikes, and high-wheeled hot-rods. The observation tower and gracefully arched belvedere on Sutro Heights long ago crumbled away, but the much-remodeled Cliff House can be seen at the left.

Six girls in stylish bathing suits make unconvincing preparations to flop into wet sand below the Cliff House in a 1914 classic of automotive ballyhoo. The car: a shiny new Chalmers. Recently, the location and costume have been taken over by paddleboard surfers in wet-suits, who warm up around a driftwood fire after hours in the water.

The first Cliff House, built during the Civil War, attracted the carriage trade until the Comstock silver bonanza ran out and a crowd of earthy politicos and camp followers flocked in.

The present Cliff House is a much-remodeled version of the third. Like its predecessors it dispenses food and drink, postcards, souvenirs, and views of plump brown sea lions.

The second Cliff House, a seven-story Bavarian castle, rose out of the ashes of the first in 1896. The "gingerbread palace" served champagne, pressed duck, and mussels à la bordelaise *to visiting presidents and local robber barons, and it survived the 1906 earthquake. The next year, it was devoured by fire.*

The Cliff at the End of the Continent

The first Cliff House (1863–94) was famous for assignations and brandy punches; the second (1896–1907), for assignations and champagne. The third and present Cliff House (1908, with lapses for Prohibition, Depression, and remodeling) is not at the moment famous for anything except its breathtaking setting, its longevity (twice that of any previous occupant of the perch), and the peculiar feeling of melancholy it induces in older San Franciscans: a sense of loss not only of what was but of what might have been.

Mark Twain, a major liar, wrote in 1864 that the Cliff House was "perched on the very brink of the ocean like a castle beside the Rhine." As one can see from the picture on the upper left, it was neither castle-like nor Rhenish. There always has been this element of hype about the Cliff, even to the reputation of its Steller's sea lions, one of which was known in the 1870s as "Ben Butler"—not for the Union general who oppressed New Orleans but for an overbearing New York Democrat. A frosty young woman from Boston, impervious to touristic attractions, wrote home saying that Ben Butler and the others on Seal Rocks "resembled nothing so much as great brown maggots writhing on a mound of porridge."

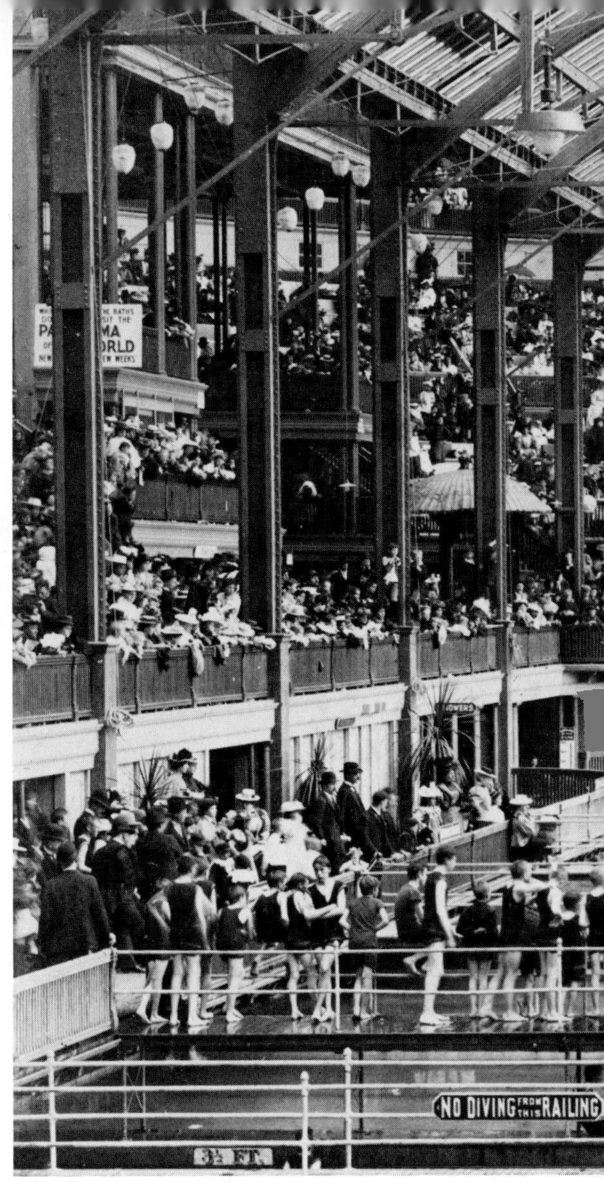

While the Sutro Band boomed out Rossini overtures and schoolchildren (admission five cents each) pranced around a pair of maypoles, seven thousand parents cheered from the misty upper galleries at the first annual May Day festival in 1897. On weekends and holidays, Sutro's Tropic Beach gave prizes for trick diving, fast swimming, fancy dancing, and bobbing after plates. Promotions—and upkeep—declined after the death of Sutro and his daughter, Dr. Emma Merritt.

Mr. Sutro's Magnificent Plunge

In an era that favored grandeur, Adolph Sutro liked to do Big Things, like digging a four-mile tunnel to drain hot water out of the mine shafts of the Comstock Lode, buying up most of the raw land in San Francisco, collecting a priceless library of rare books and incunabula, and building (in 1896) what he called the World's Largest Indoor Swimming Pool at the very edge of the world's largest ocean.

Although it was uglier than a tin barn, Sutro's Baths and Museum charmed visitors with contests, curios, and six kinds of bathing (salt, fresh, warm, cold, deep, shallow). Declining patronage in the 1950s forced the owners to sell off the museum, close all but one pool, and install an ice rink. In the early '60s they closed the doors and sold the site to an apartment developer. Shortly afterward, fire destroyed the building and the city acquired the land for open space.

Like the gray knit suits it used to rent, Sutro's went out of style. All that remains is dismal masonry, crumbling like the ruins of a ravaged fortress.

Museum was part Barnum, part pack-rat: clockwork dolls, Egyptian mummies, marble statuary, potted palms, and a moth-eaten menagerie of stuffed animals.

Generations of San Franciscans learned at Sutro's to plunge down long slides, flip from trapezes, dive from steel rafters—even to swim.

Sunday in the Park

When Golden Gate Park passed its hundredth anniversary a few years ago, several rude critics suggested that the old dear was getting obsolete.

What a reaction! Our beloved bedside garden *obsolete!*—with its forest of rhododendrons in the spring, its meadows flecked with English daisies, its funky bandstand among the pollarded sycamores, its human love-ins, its clouds of marijuana floating over like an ermine cape—our park *obsolete?*

And yet . . . Much as we do revere the memory of William Hammond Hall, who contrived the plan to capture more than a thousand acres of red rock and dunes, and that of his successor, John McLaren, who supervised the greening of the sands for fifty-six years until his death, at ninety-six, in 1943, they both were men of the nineteenth century, raised in a world of horse-drawn buggies, horticultural displays, and Suppé overtures. Hall had in mind the Bois de Boulogne, its carriage drives and stylish promenades; McLaren dreamed of the feudal English country estates where he had learned gardening. The park they built is ill-adapted to rummage sales, museum expansion, automobile traffic, rock concerts, political demonstrations, drug use, bus tours, carnival rides, gang warfare, and such functions as it now fulfills.

Should a park reflect the heritage of the past, the fashions of the present, or the needs of the future? For more than three decades, ever since John McLaren died, the city has avoided the question. Bequests of former benefactors (buildings, lakes, waterfalls) have deteriorated. Instant uses (roads, parking lots, a sewage treatment plant, an ugly exhibit hall) have intruded. Future requirements have been ignored. Meanwhile, through a thousand Sundays, the park and the people have been getting together in joyful disharmony, changing each other for better, for worse.

Bench-sitting, a civilized alternative to fidgety sports, is popular today as in the 1880s and is performed in precisely the same manner. Technology has not improved on park benches or parasols, although science has brought us aluminum tube chairs. A Dutch windwill (below), an intriguing destination for a carriage ride in 1902, was built that year in the northwest corner of the park to pump fresh water to reservoirs from wells only three hundred yards from the ocean.

Barefoot dancing, an ecstatic alternative to bench-sitting, lures disciples of Sufi mysticism to a piney meadow for several hours of dervish-like whirling on a weekend in the 1970s. "You see?" a spectator observed. "Anything draws a crowd nowadays." Lawn bowling has attracted a cult of Sunday athletes for decades; roller skating, like dervish calisthenics, is a recent fancy.

A Swinging Time at Grandfather's Place

For more than ninety years a secluded corner of Golden Gate Park quaintly named the Children's Quarters has made claim to being the oldest juvenile playground in a public park in the United States. It looks its age. The sandstone battlements of Sharon Cottage glower above a field of gray and mottled asphalt. The baby farm animals live in the rural simplicity of pioneer America. Over at the sand pile, some boys are climbing and descending, climbing and descending a corkscrew slide once polished by their grandfathers' breeches.

Worse than the aging is the ugly evidence of a changed society: the tawdry carnival rides; the precocious extortionists roaming in gangs, extracting pocket money from guileless victims; the neglected buildings and decaying playthings that a wealthy city somehow cannot afford to maintain.

But the tastes of children are undemanding and invariable. Slippery ramps with bumps and wiggles, seesaw swings, a cable car to climb on, a carousel that plays recorded music as the gilded hippodrome turns circles mirrored in eternity—such are the Sunday joys, today as they were in 1886. Like peppermint drops and saltwater taffy, the playground has been improved upon but never quite supplanted.

Dizzy, stomach-dropping flight down the giant corkscrew charms a Disneyland-jaded generation just as it did their grandparents in the quiet years before World War I.

A romanesque "cottage," a gift of U. S. Senator William Sharon, opened in 1886 as a family restaurant. Recently used as a furniture storehouse and a hot-dog stand, the building was gutted by fire in April 1974, partially restored after several years of neglect. An animal farm was started in 1941 to let city-bound kids pet lambs, guinea pigs, and poultry.

To the young, the playground's old-fashioned amusements—fresh as life itself.

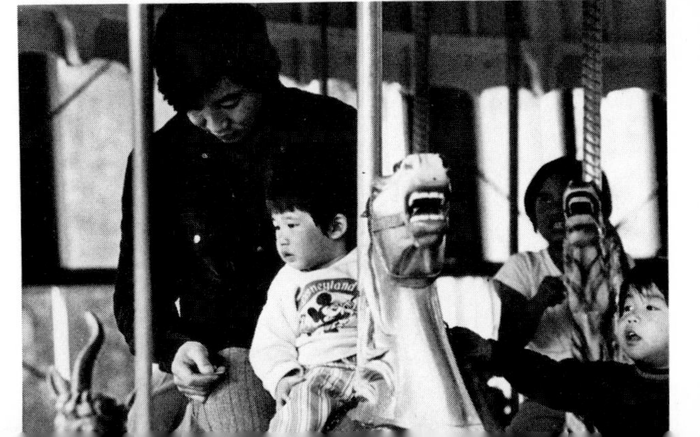

A Souvenir Made in Japan

The most attractive novelty at the California Midwinter International Exposition in Golden Gate Park in 1894 was not, as one might suppose, the first motorcar in San Francisco, the first bloomer girls, the Edison electric light, the John Philip Sousa band, or even Little Egypt and Her Notorious Danse du Ventre, *di-rect* from the World's Columbian Exposition in Chicago, Illinois. It was (we are reliably informed) the Japanese Village, a four-acre garden of dwarf trees, fishponds, odd little bridges, and torii gates, presided over by young women in kimonos and fancy haircombs.

Visitors in 1894 found geishas—or what they hoped were geishas—loitering under a fragile canopy that floated above the Moon Bridge. Most structures in the Japanese Tea Garden have been remodeled or replaced over the past eighty years, but the two-story wooden torii gate at the main entrance dates from the Midwinter Exposition. Among the fairgoers below is a Chinese wearing the traditional queue.

While other mementos of the fair have disappeared and Little Egypt has been gathered among the pharaohs, the Japanese Village has endured, first as the Japanese Tea Garden; then, during a decade of patriotic yahooism amid and after World War II, as the "Oriental" Tea Garden; and now as the Japanese Tea Garden, all over again.

George T. Marsh, an importer of Asian art, designed and built the original with materials and workmen from Japan, and for more than thirty years the family of one of the workers, Makoto Hagiwara, ran the tea-and-almond-cookie concession and maintained the garden at a rental of fifty dollars a month. Faced with internment in 1942, the Hagiwaras, to the chagrin of the Park Department, disposed of their collection of stone lanterns, bonsai trees, and flowering shrubs. Many of these, through the bequest of Dr. Hugh Fraser, eventually found their way back to San Francisco, where, with other gifts, redevelopments, plantations, and expansions, they have contributed to the beauty, celebrity, and population of the Tea Garden.

Traffic congeals on the Moon Bridge on weekends, especially when cherry blossoms, magnolias, and azaleas are in bloom. Wishful thinking has transformed the arch into "Wishing Bridge," from which a penny thrown is a fortune earned. Present inhabitants of the garden include concessionaires, goldfish, and goldfish-eating raccoons.

The ten-foot bronze Buddha with hand raised in a benign gesture of abhaya *(freedom from fear) poses for its umpteenth portrait in three decades. A gift to the city from Gump's store, the statue was cast in 1790 in Tajima Province, where it was called "the-Buddha-that-sits-through-sunny-and-rainy-weather-without-shade."*

Admirals of the Inland Seas

In the golden days when sailboats moved by wind alone and ladies carried parasols and let men paddle the canoe, Golden Gate Park acquired two small but navigable bodies of water of indisputable charm: doughtnut-shaped Stow Lake, a mile-round moat at the base of Strawberry Hill; and pear-shaped (or South America-shaped) Spreckels Lake, a seven-acre pewter platter lying by the Main Drive at Thirty-sixth Avenue.

Stow, which was scooped out and flooded in 1893, always has been a rowers' lake, a magnet to bo'sun's mates on liberty and high school kids on marijuana. No white water (it's only three or four feet deep), just pampas grass and paddle wheels and the beady scrutiny of an occasional sea gull floating by. Spreckels, the model-makers' pond, is a divided jurisdiction, administered like a colonial province by the San Francisco Model Yacht Club. On alternate weekends it is reserved for sailing vessels and for power craft. It is always easy to tell whose day it is: you can hear the power boats breaking the sonic barrier five blocks away.

Watchful sailors used bamboo wands to guide their delicate craft on a Sunday morning a few years after Spreckels Lake and its yacht club were created in 1900. A modern skipper (left) directs his boat from shore by radio signals.

Since the first oarsmen made the circuit in wooden rowboats in the '90s, electric launches and knee-action swan boats have come to Stow Lake. The lake serves as a park reservoir, but an artificial waterfall stopped running in 1962.

A Spin in the Park

Golden Gate Park began, in a sense, as a carriage drive—a thick green ribbon stretching from the center of the city out to the lonely dunes. In the 1880s, when the young men of San Francisco took up the international craze for big-wheeled "ordinaries," biking clubs rolled into the park like invading armies, although "scorchers" who frightened horses by exceeding the six-mile-an-hour speed limit were subject to a hundred-dollar fine.

Since then, two-wheeled and four-wheeled vehicles have disputed the territory. Currently, after fifty years of subjugation to the automobile, bikers are again in the driver's seat.

Arrival of an open touring car at the Stow Lake boathouse heralded the auto invasion of the park in the decade after World War I.

Siamese-twin bicycles with a baby seat between stopped other bikers in their tracks in 1898. Women cyclists, whose long skirts had precluded their riding the big-wheeled "ordinaries," easily handled the new "safety bicycles" of the '90s.

The safety bicycle had a low center of gravity, prototype of today's bikes. In 1895 an eighteen-pound Rambler No. 10, "Fastest on Earth," sold for seventy dollars.

NATIONAL MARITIME MUSEUM AT SAN FRANCISCO

Revival of biking in the 1970s brings cyclists of every age to Golden Gate Park. Rental shops offer five-speeds, ten-speeds, tandems, baby carriers. A portion of John F. Kennedy Drive, the main east-west route, is closed to motor vehicles on Sundays, creating a bike trail the length of the park.

A Growing Appetite for Pigskin

All cities, especially crowded, indoorsy cities like San Francisco, breed athletic teams, and teams breed spectators. We have been producing both, in our casual way, ever since the resident Mexicans at Mission Dolores taught the gold hunters of '49 to bet on bull-bear fights and bareback horse races.

Nothing is more changeable, however, than the taste of the public for games. Football, which now dominates our weekends from late summer to midwinter, was literally unknown here ninety years ago. Basketball trickled in as a YMCA diversion for kids who were too skinny for football. Tennis was an amusement for snooty young women. Skiing was done by Scandinavians on barrel staves. Golf was for Scots in tweeds. When the Olympic Club, which now calls itself the oldest and second largest urban sports club in America, was formed in 1860, it offered only calisthenics, fencing, and trapeze. Those were *athletics,* not to be confused with *sports,* the coarse, vaguely immoral pastimes of gamblers, volunteer firemen, and women of frolicsome disposition.

It was football, an insidiously democratic spectacle, that brought sports into athletics, and vice versa, by blending organized brutality with the social cachet of Yale University. Football came to San Francisco in 1892, when Stanford and the University of California played their first challenge match on a grassy plot off Stanyan Street. Within a few years, even the Olympic Club was fielding a football team, primitive prelude to the mania of today's enthusiasts who drive their RV's to the Oakland Coliseum, spread out a tailgate picnic, then retire inside the van to watch the Raiders on TV.

National Football League 49ers, franchised in 1946 as members of the newly formed "All-America Football Conference," have played since 1971 at Candlestick Park, one of the few sports stadiums accessible by boat.

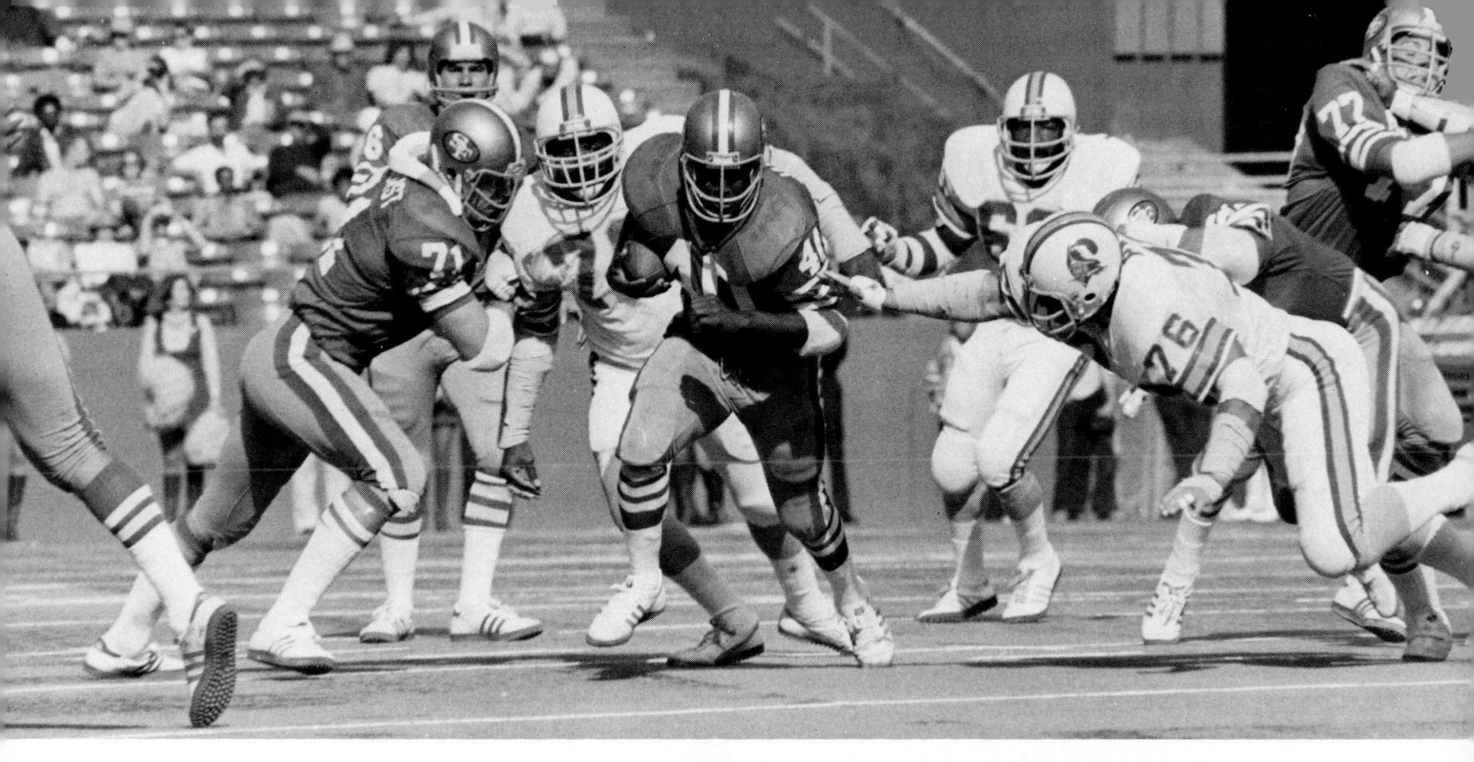

Left: Stanford's 5–0 win over California in 1900 was blighted by tragedy. The roof of a factory adjoining the field at Sixteenth and Folsom Streets collapsed under freeloading spectators, plunging hundreds of men and boys onto white-hot glass furnaces. Two dozen died of injuries. Players and equipment—as well as bleachers—are sturdier at Candlestick.

Followed by teammates in a flying wedge (center right), an unidentified ball carrier risks concussion for glory in the 1901 Big Game at Folsom Street Recreation Park (California 2, Stanford 0). The game was moved to Cal's home field in 1904, and thereafter has alternated annually between Berkeley and Palo Alto, with interruptions for rugby (1906–14) and war. Right: Bucking the Denver line at Candlestick in 1977, 49er running back Paul Hofer has his flying wedge up front in the person of Wilbur Jackson.

The Giants' (at that time) Tim Foli accepts a pat and a handshake from second baseman Rob Andrews for lighting up the home run sign during a generally lackluster 1977 season. Below: Willie McCovey slides home to score against the Atlanta Braves.

Going Big League

For pure nostalgia, nothing can touch the Good Old Seals, our Pacific Coast League baseball team from 1903 to 1958, when we divorced them to take up with a runaway from Manhattan. Their very names are a litany: Smead Jolley, Earl Averill, Gus Suhr, "Lefty" O'Doul, Willie Kamm, "Ping" Bodie, Frank Crosetti, the DiMaggios . . .

Before the Seals, local base ball teams (three words in those days) were "clubs" in more than name. The champions were the Haverlys, an Irish outfit, mostly, except for a kid named Levy at right field. They played the Pioneers, the Wasps, and the Hornets. We couldn't wait to get out of that league, into our own Far Western imitation of the majors.

Seals Stadium, "The Green Queen," opened in 1931. It had a barber's chair in the dressing room, a live seal in a tank, a glass backstop behind home plate. Every year the best players "went up" to the majors, became world famous, and were seen here no more. (That was the trouble with being in a minor league. We figured it was different in the majors.)

To be second string—especially when the reason was a geographic accident—was something no American city could accept. When the Giants

In a rare action photograph from the 1890s, an unidentified Oakland batter crosses home plate standing up.

winked, we swooned, built a stadium, danced in the streets. Almost 1,800,000 fans turned out the first year at Candlestick Park. Two years later, the Giants took the pennant.

Things never have been as good again. Is it TV? The A's in Oakland? A dying sport? Suddenly, for pure nostalgia, nothing touches the Good Old Seals.

Recreation Park at Fifteenth and Harrison Streets, where the Seals played from 1907 to 1930, was known for its short right field, splintery bleachers, and "booze cage," where beer was five cents, whiskey ten cents, advice on improving your game free.

Father and Sons Night in April 1950, packed sixteen-thousand-seat Seals Stadium at Sixteenth and Bryant. The Seals attracted 670,563 fans to home games in one season (1946)—better than the National League Giants have done some years at 56,000-seat Candlestick Park.

The California Comet, and Other Nearby Planets

Although it is the least provincial of sports—a contest of blazing individuality, often played across international lines—tennis was for several decades a source of intense local pride in the San Francisco Bay Area. We nurtured a generation of winners in the 1920s and '30s, and we were quite willing to attribute them to our climate, our frontier manners, our citrus fruit, our genes, our asphalt courts—anything that would justify our basking in the sportswriters' unoriginal epithet "Cradle of Champions."

Tennis, like other civilizing influences, came late to northern California, reeking of Eastern snobbery and social caste. From the mid-1870s, when the modern game was invented, to the start of World War I, most national champions trained on the shaved lawns of Newport, Nahant, or Germantown, and collegiate tennis was dominated by Harvard, Yale and Princeton. Finally, San Francisco made the game safe for democracy by turning it over to high school kids who learned on public courts in Golden Gate Park.

When Maurice McLoughlin broke into the top ranks of American tennis in 1909 (they called him the California Comet), he credited his slashing serve and aggressive net attack to the park's cement courts. During the next several decades, so many Californians demonstrated this concrete advantage that our provincial chauvinism was satiated. Hardly anyone cares nowadays that Rosie Casals gives an address in Sausalito or that Billie Jean King (sometimes) calls San Mateo home. (Tennis players are always traveling, anyway.) The important question is, how long's the waiting list for this court?

Left: "Little Bill" Johnston won national singles title in 1915 from fellow-San Franciscan Maurice McLoughlin, then fought for one-two position for the next ten years with "Big Bill" Tilden. Solemn, visor-capped Helen Wills Moody ("Miss Poker Face") of Berkeley (near right) won eight Wimbledon and seven Forest Hills crowns, finally was defeated (1932) by another Berkeley girl, her arch-rival Helen Jacobs, who in turn succumbed to Alice Marble (center right) of San Francisco. A formidable backhand carried Don Budge (far right) from Berkeley to championships in the United States, Britain, and Australia in the late 1930s.

While playing doubles on a dirt court in the East Bay ninety years ago (left), ladies wore hats, gloves, and bustles, and gentlemen kindly avoided cannonball serves. Women's doubles at a recent Virginia Slims Tournament in Civic Auditorium paired Chris Evert and Billie Jean King (off camera) against Rosie Casals and Nancy Gunther (far court), with bare legs and bullet serves both in fashion.

The eight-meter Yucca *bears southeastward from the Golden Gate in the San Francisco Cup series on an afternoon in the mid-1970s.*

Days on the Bay

To every sailor in northern California since the Costanoan Indians, life in San Francisco has centered on the 450 square miles of landlocked water called the bay. It never was a paradise for three-seat barges woven of tule grass or ten-foot Whitehall boats with dripping canvas sails. But where there is moisture there will be small craft, despite high winds, strong tides, and treacherous shoals. The San Francisco Yacht Club was formed in 1869, the Pacific Yacht Club ten years later, the Corinthian in 1886.

If the bay was forbidding to the smallest boats, it was challenging to the largest. In the nineteenth century, hay scows and lumber schooners, Chinese junks and Italian feluccas wallowed around the islands in multi-class international regattas for such booty as a ton of coal. Lately, the hulls are fiber glass, the sails are colored spinnakers, the prizes are trophy cups; but the allure of wind and water is much as it was when Commodore Isador Gutte used to race the *Chispa* up to Carquinez Strait of a Sunday afternoon, with liberal potations to cut the chill.

A party of Sunday picnickers in the 1880s kept their lightly rigged mosquito boat Caprice *within the shelter of the Marin shore.*

Two-masted schooners, the utility craft of the coastal trade when sailing was a business as well as a sport, lay at anchor off Black Point, just inside the Gate, on a winter evening in the 1880s.

Prize-winning Racy, *a Peterson two-ton fiber-glass craft, sails on a reach toward a marker east of Angel Island during one of the St. Francis Yacht Club's series of cup races for big boats in September 1976.*

California Jockey Club, a winter resort for the sporting crowd in 1898, occupied a 160-acre park atop an ancient Indian shell mound on the edge of the bay in Emeryville. Opened in 1861, the shell mound park was leveled for a factory site in 1924.

Every Man a King

Around these democratic parts it never has been a sport of kings—more like a sport of robber barons—but the racing of thoroughbreds and trotting horses long has appealed to the Bay Area crowd, aristocratic or not. A hustler from New York laid out the first track in the Mission District during the gold rush, and within a few years gamblers were importing horses from Australia to compete in weekend sweepstakes.

Railroad and mining millionaires built private tracks in Millbrae and Menlo Park and bred racing stock in stables with mahogany paneling and crystal chandeliers. The really grand spenders—Senator George Hearst, Leland Stanford, James Ben Ali Haggin—sponsored public tracks where ordinary toffs and touts could drop their modest fortunes. The tradition continues each fall at Bay Meadows (San Mateo County) and each spring at Golden Gate Fields, where on a California Derby Day a few years back the pari-mutuel machines recorded $2,291,576 in wagers, not a dime of it placed by a king.

Daniel "White Hat" McCarty, a former horse trainer who made a fortune on a single bet, wore his eponymous headgear while showing off a light harness rig at the Bay District Track in the 1890s. Right: Jockey Roy Selden, the juvenile hero of the Bay Area, in winner's circle at Emeryville, 1911, and Johnny Longden, of more recent fame, on "Noor" after a world-record 1¼ miles (1:58:1) at Golden Gate Fields in 1950.

Golden Gate Fields (top), on the east edge of the bay at Albany, holds thoroughbred races February through June, including thirty-five days sponsored by Tanforan Racing Association, whose sixty-four-year-old-track (center) in San Bruno burned down in 1963. Tanforan is now a shopping center with a racehorse logo.

HOT
HIPPODROME
THALIA
SPIDER
KELLY
HIPPO=
=DROME
OPEN TO ALL COMERS

CHAPTER 9

The Good Life and the Bad

A Yukon sourdough, recalling how he spent his first poke of gold dust from the creeks of Circle, Alaska, looked back with a wistful smile upon a certain day in August 1896:

"We landed at Frisco and stopped at the Western Hotel. My, how glad we were to get there! We went out on the sidewalk and looked around at the big buildings—a stranger in a strange land. The people on the sidewalk were just as thick as the mosquitos at Circle City . . .

"We went to a theater, then to a dance hall, then to see a big fighter named John L. Sullivan. Then across the street but not to bed yet. After I got in bed, I heard shots and saw two men lying in the street and the next day saw in the paper that two Chinamen were shot on Kearny Street. It made me wish I was back in the Yukon . . .

"Next night the gang from the Yukon went down 'South of the Slot' and had a hot time. Those girls made the squaws and Circle City dance hall girls look like a Dirty Deuce in a new deck. But they came high . . ."

Now, it should not be inferred that everyone who visits San Francisco seeks (or finds) such carnal pleasures. That is why so many Citizens of Good Repute objected when a mayor some years back bragged that San Francisco was the Paris of the West. They suspected him of making a salacious innuendo. But the mayor, who knew the value of equivocation, went right on drawing grandiose comparisons, even suggesting that the day was coming when Paris would be called the San Francisco of Europe.

Pacific Street (left) was called "Terrific Street" in the early years of this century. Today the action has moved a block north to Broadway, but the base instincts are the same.

Dinner in Town

The favorite hedonistic diversion of visitors and residents in San Francisco, and the only one open to persons of every age, is eating in restaurants. A group of executives, when asked recently to compare the attractions of several American cities, said that they preferred the restaurants of San Francisco to those of any other place on the list and, what's more, preferred San Francisco's restaurants to anything else the city offered in the way of climate, dwellings, or playthings.

This speaks well for a city which in its infancy served up fried murre eggs from the offshore rocks, moldy potatoes from the Sandwich Islands, and well-aged grizzly bear steaks from the Sierra Nevada, all at extortionate prices, to a captive clientele. Credit for improving the bill of fare goes in part to the temperate climate, which the executives discounted, and to the seaside situation, which they overlooked, for these endowed us with an abundance of seafoods, salad greens, fresh fruits, and dry wines that are not produced in, say, Wichita. (The bay and coastal waters are depleted now, fruits and vegetables are frozen, and wines are sent in tanker ships to thirsty ports on the Atlantic, diminishing our geographic advantage; but a head start helps.)

More important than natural resources were immigrants from Europe. The French have never been numerous here, but they use their talents well and bring along recipes; the Italians are both numerous and talented; and, in recent years, new immigrants from Asia have brought tempura, rijsttafel, papadams, and hot-sour soup into a menu and vocabulary already rich in osso bucco, piroshki, and coquilles St. Jacques.

The Garden Court of the Sheraton Palace Hotel, designed by architect George Kelham on the site of the carriage court of the original Palace Hotel, is one of the world's handsomest dining rooms—and one of few designated a historic landmark.

Your favorite little restaurant is not something to noise around, especially in print. We feel safe in publicizing this free buffet, however, because you will no longer find the like of it this side of heaven. As for Larachet's, it, too, is past being spoiled, having disappeared into glory in the 1890s. They were said to serve a first-rate chicken dinner, wine included, for under a dollar.

Sunday dinner at New Delmonico on Geary Street in the 1890s included a generous platter of succulent little bay shrimp (ah, where are they now?), a bottle of the house wine, and a serenade by a string trio in the music loft. Despite such ravishments, a few of the young patrons show evidence of Sunday ennui.

DIANA HALL
SPIDER KELLY
THALIA
PURCELL'S
THE MIDWAY
SCHLITZ 5¢
U.S.

ARABIAN NIGHTS
ARABIAN NIGHTS
INTERNATIONAL SETTLEMENT
LUCCA
FRISKY
JUST TELL THE MAN YOU WANT IMPERIAL!
INTERNATIONAL SETTLEMENT
Lucca's Family DINNER
Open
KEARNY

DO NOT ENTER
Take a Goose to lunch.
SAVOY AUTO
PARKING
DO NOT ENTER

Ghost of the Coast

The Barbary Coast, known in popular journalism as the *notorious* Barbary Coast, was the gold-lined underbelly of San Francisco's commercial life for half a century before Prohibition—"a Maelstrom of Sin," said one of the papers, aglow with provincial pride. It was a well-marked, accessible district where a visitor had limitless opportunity to drink watered whiskey, dance the tango, acquire an Unspeakable Disease, or have the side of his head laid open with a bung starter, all without danger of wandering into the residential neighborhoods.

Having always catered to animal cravings and moral weaknesses, San Francisco made it a civic policy to provide a larger and better equipped Cesspool of Indecency (as editorialists fondly termed it) than did most other cities. Basically, the Coast was only one block of Pacific (billed in the '90s as "Terrific") Street, between Kearny and Montgomery. But its wicked influence permeated the whole area from Chinatown to the waterfront, from Broadway to Clay Street. Although no one ever audited the books, the Coast must have been vastly more profitable than any other industry on the Pacific slope, not only to its owners and protectors, but also to what are nowadays called "related service businesses."

What has become of it, this Resort of High Revel so obviously suited to contemporary tastes? Was it really swept away in a surge of municipal virtue stirred up by the Hearst newspapers in anticipation of the 1915 exposition? Did Prohibition kill it? Or did it expire of boredom with its own monotonous and unimaginative depravity?

Perhaps the Coast never was as bad (or good) as it has been painted and is in fact alive and living in those smoky, disappointing body shows along Broadway, where even now the police perform occasional "raids," invariably discovering people doing illegal things to one another with every evidence of continued and unrepentant pleasure.

Metamorphosis of Pacific Avenue (née Street) from a row of dives into a row of advertising agencies and interior decorators' studios illustrates the redemptive power of sandblasting, zoning, and a shortage of cheap office space. Top (1913): Spider Kelly's, the Thalia, and Purcell's shamelessly took credit for infecting American youth with the Turkey Trot, the Bunny Hug, and the Grizzly Bear. Center (1930s): The Coast tried a post-Prohibition comeback as the International Settlement, which sounded vaguely erotic. Its most popular enterprise was Lucca's, with six-course dinners at one dollar. Bottom (1970s): Cloaked in virtue and Indian fig laurel trees, the street has forgotten Oofty-Goofty, Mother Bronson, and the Galloping Cow. Ave atque vale.

Hard as they try, the clubs on Broadway never succeed in looking as perilous as the old Coast. In 1946 (below) many of the bars on Pacific were off-limits to naval personnel, a stigma that hurt a few of the proprietors economically but gave the neighborhood an evil magnetism, allowing the Coast to rejoice in a few last years of authentic ill-repute.

The Kingston Trio won their first success in the early 1950s at Enrico Banducci's hungry i, a basement club in North Beach. Unpretentious, uncomfortable, and inexpensive, the i perfected a style of intimate music and topical comedy that lured a thin but influential audience away from TV and gave a start to such as Mort Sahl, Lenny Bruce, Stan Wilson, the Limeliters, Woody Allen, and Irwin Corey.

Led by a bosomy, middle-aged male named Lucien in the role of Sophie Tucker, Finocchio's "Parisian Review" of thirty years ago played the same dress-up game that has titillated busloads of tourists for decades: "Is he or isn't she?" Lower right: An impudent poster proclaims the reaction of one Broadway club to a recent city campaign against provocative outdoor advertising.

Nocturnal Diversions

Few cities have enjoyed San Francisco's almost uninterrupted success in maintaining a reputation for depravity-after-dark. Sodom and Gomorrah come to mind, but they achieved divine publicity.

During the gold rush, the city was a world-class gambling hell. Later, when municipal and state authorities interfered with games of chance, venereal enterprises took over: crib houses, parlor houses, peep shows, bestiality. After the earthquake-fire had leveled the celebrated red-light districts, dance halls emerged that shocked the parsonages of

Melodeon of a century ago served up avant-garde European amusements to a select audience of miners, seamen, and townies. The Barbary Coast dance hall below illustrated San Francisco's "vivid sinfulness" in an 1873 book on the wicked West. "Percentage girls," whose original sin was dancing for pay, continued the vile tradition at Spider Kelly's in 1911, joined by Little Egypt, one of innumerable nautch dancers who shared a name originated in Chicago in the '90s.

America with coeducational acrobatics imported from the bawdy quarters of the Argentine.

There have been lean times with the fat: Prohibition turned off the essential lubricants, television drained away the customers. But even in slow seasons, when the nightly offerings dwindled to transvestites, satire, and topless waitresses, San Francisco held its rank as a matrix of naughty new ideas, most of which have rapidly spread to other cities that would never have allowed them in the first place.

Little Women

Back when bastardy was rated a social disadvantage and polite San Franciscans would not have attended a costume party called "The Hookers' Ball," a scrap of doggerel went the rounds of the cabarets:

The miners came in forty-nine
The whores in fifty-one;
When they got together,
They produced the native son.

It is dismaying to consider how many persons may have inferred from this nasty rhyme that prostitution is only the *second* oldest profession in California. To the contrary, prostitution was well established here by 1846, if not considerably earlier, and may have even predated the arrival of the aboriginal California Indians, whenever that occurred.

The following things are known about prostitution in San Francisco:

1. Most prostitutes on the old Barbary Coast were female, and most of their customers were male.
2. Many prostitutes nowadays are not female, and neither are their customers.
3. Most prostitutes, past and present, have been either white, black, brown, yellow, red, or combinations thereof.
4. Prostitution historically has been confined to North Beach, Chinatown, downtown, Nob and Russian Hills, the Richmond, Sunset, Mission, Bayview, South of Market, Western Addition, and Haight districts.
5. Prostitution is believed by many persons to result from poverty, dependence on drugs, poor education, lack of effective birth control methods, ease of birth control, weak law enforcement, pornography, absence of family discipline, affluence, heredity, foreign immigration, low community moral standards, racial discrimination, sexual inhibition, militarism, religious bigotry, exploitation of women by men, temptation of men by women, birth trauma, and several other causes.
6. For reasons beyond the scope of this book, outbursts of public indignation against mercenary sexual activities are closely related to political campaigns, newspaper circulation drives, and efforts to improve the audience rating of the evening news.
7. Between the writing and publication of this summary, the San Francisco police will have raided at least one "thriving bordello," news of which will occasion letters to the editor complaining that San Francisco is a moral quagmire and that the cops should not waste their time enforcing laws against the sexual activities of consenting adults.

If the authors appear to be making light of a serious subject, they apologize. Their intention is exactly the opposite.

This portrait of a madam and her "girls" has been frequently published to illuminate the horrors of the Coast. A scholar of California history has cast doubt on its authenticity, however, alleging that it was a student hoax and actually pictures the 1890 pledge class of a sorority at the University of California.

Immigrant girls disembarking at New York's Castle Garden in the early 1880s were advised to beware of multi-armed matrons who would sell them into lives of shame on the Barbary Coast (above). Meanwhile, out in San Francisco, a weekly paper viewed the social evil from a different perspective, titling this cartoon, "How Officer Price and Other Policemen Make Money."

To Each His Own

A friend of ours who is far along in the pigeonhole school of social science has begun an elaborate classification of the bars of San Francisco. Beginning with Windowless-Heterosexual-Ethnic-Neighborhood-Pinball Playgrounds, he has progressed upward to Major-Regional-Carpeted Touristic Monuments like the Equinox Room of the Hyatt Regency, which revolves 360 degrees during the average time required to consume one strawberry daiquiri.

Our friend has identified Nostalgia-Exploitation bars, Sado-Masochistic Friendship Clubs, Irish Revolutionary Cells, Media Outlets, Meat Racks, Specialty Shops ("Try Our Fermented Afghani Mare's Milk Punch"), and several bona fide Guild Halls, including the Crab Fishermen's Grotto and the Wholesale Florists' Bower. His tentative conclusion is that there is a type of bar for every type of San Franciscan. To complete his thesis, he needs only to classify the significant varieties of San Franciscans inhabiting our urban jungle, a task that he expects will require at least a decade and several federal grants.

At a recent count, San Francisco embraced some 1,116 establishments dispensing liquor on premises, 1,056 selling spirits to take out, and 1,080 offering wine and beer. This provides a source of supply for every 200 residents, including children, and, to paraphrase one of our late political leaders, it comes within a few figures of being a vast and tremendous number.

Conditions were not ever thus. When saloon-drinking was exclusively a male sport and aguardiente was measured out in a bull's horn, San Francisco had only high-class saloons, low-class sa-

Henry Africa's (above) is a category-breaker, being simultaneously a tourist monument, mixer, and neighborhood pub. Tommy's Joynt (below) in the style of Dick's Saloon at the turn of the century, attracts drop-ins to its steam buffet at Geary and Van Ness by emblazoning its walls with turkey carcasses and steins of lager.

loons, and dives. Variety, or the simulacrum of variety, is a characteristic of recent times. Whether it makes us richer or happier is a subject for bar-stool discourse, however, not for this narrow space. Nor is this the place to deal with the problems of heavy drinking and alcoholism that are implicit in our lush abundance of groggeries. These problems occur, alas, not only in saloons but in kitchens, parks, hotel rooms, hospitals, and grit-blown alleys.

Election night circa 1905 in an all-purpose, all-male saloon of the Irish persuasion brings together enthusiasts of the Feeley-for-Assembly campaign for a glass of stout and a bagpipe concert. The roadhouse below, at what is now Forty-third Avenue and Geary Boulevard, offered refreshment in 1903 to thirsty wayfarers en route from the city to the ocean beach along the Point Lobos carriage-and-gas-buggy road.

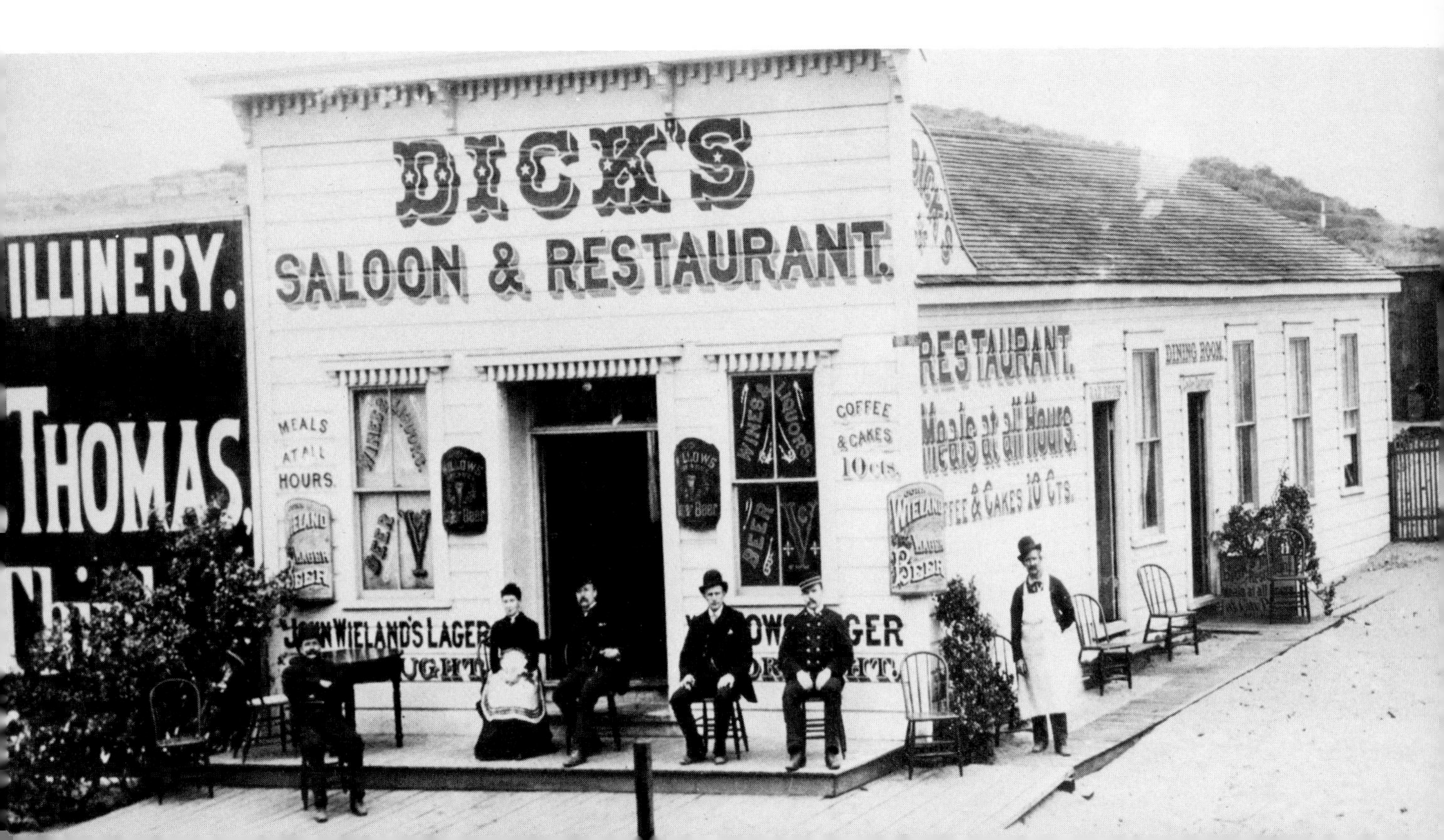

The True Home Brew

Nowadays, they call it an "acquired taste"—dark and malty, heavy on hops, and, to some palates, rather flat. Back in the sudsy '90s, no fewer than twenty-seven San Francisco breweries were turning out steam beer, a unique California product mothered by necessity. A single plant survives, resisting current fashions and corporate mergers by appealing to curiosity, nostalgia, and a cult of steam beer fanatics.

No, it is not made with steam nor served at the

boiling point. The name describes the pressure of natural fermentation, which bursts in a fragrant cloud from a freshly tapped keg.

Steam beer is fermented and aged in San Francisco's normally cool air temperatures instead of the refrigerated chill of traditional lagering. Thirsty pioneers invented this unusual brewing technique to beat the high price of importing beer around the Horn or bringing ice from Sitka, Alaska.

About its flavor: Columnist Charles McCabe rates steam beer as one of two American brews worth tasting. (The other, says he, is Rainier ale.) But a pair of magazine writers who recently sampled beers across the country found steam beer "one more instance of San Francisco's chronic confusion of eccentricity with quality." *De gustibus* (etc.).

Immigration and refrigeration had brought German lagering to the West by the 1890s, when this jolly Teutonic crew lined up for a company portrait. But the United States Brewery, like Enrico Migheli's roadhouse, on the way to San Jose (left), continued to purvey sharp steam along with porter, lager, and stout. An underage customer was licking the foam off a flagon of Mission Steam at Enrico's even as the camera clicked.

Founded in 1896, Anchor Brewery rolled thousands of kegs out of its original plant on Mission Street. Now called the Steam Beer Brewing Company, Anchor still makes its rare product in a brewery near the old site.

Above left: 1978—a pub in North Beach provides its clientele steam beer on draught and the solace of shared gloom. Below left: 1878—in the Fountain beer hall at Kearny and Sutter (John Casimir, Prop.) gentlemen did not remove their hats while sipping steam, and ladies did not intrude.

CHAPTER 10

A Persistent Taste for Art and Beauty

New cities, new countries, and new money invariably are drawn to the arts. San Francisco in the late nineteenth century was a new city in a new country, and it was rich.

The result was an occasionally embarrassing yen for Culture. Stories are told of a millionaire banker who called in an artist and commanded him to "paint me some Old Masters," and of another who confided to a touring pianist that he didn't "care much for fiddling." A pioneer dentist, having prospered on extractions, adorned the streets of San Francisco (and those of Philadelphia, San Jose, and Washington, D.C.) with sculptured drinking fountains of such repellent design (his own) that a senator from California urged the Congress to uproot them from Washington lest they be supposed to represent the level of civilization in the Far West. (Here at home, a throng of artists dealt with one of the fountains by toppling it from its pedestal and dumping it into the bay.)

In short, the nouveaux riches of the Bay Area were as unsophisticated as those of any other American city, and if San Francisco later proved to be relatively discriminating, as well as insatiable, in its thirst for opera and drama, literature and painting, that may be explained by the large number of Europeans who brought well-developed tastes and talents to an isolated frontier town.

Once aroused, our passion for the arts has endured with an intensity unusual in a city that is both young and small. As a consequence, there normally are more musicians, actors, poets, and painters hereabout than the Bay Area can support, blending their hungry voices in a chronic wail: "If San Franciscans love the arts so much, why don't they appreciate me?"

Conservative in style, modest in scale, intimate and undemanding, San Francisco's favorite outdoor statuary has run to a pattern—an unencumbered bronze bambino in the park in the 1890s, a giant snail by Beniamino Bufano at the Academy of Science in the 1970s. Ruth Asawa's cylindrical fountain at the Hyatt Hotel on Union Square (below) conforms perfectly to the tradition. With its intricate relief of whimsical urban scenes, it is pleasant, unassuming, and immensely popular.

The Penguins *(left), by Beniamino Bufano, at the Golden Gateway. At right, clockwise from nine o'clock:* Porpoise, *1906, at Alaska Commercial Building, 310 Sansome Street (recently torn down)* ; Bear, *1921, by Jo Mora, 1000 Van Ness Avenue;* Lion, *1906–11, U.S. Customs House, 555 Battery Street;* Stallion, *1909, from an Atherton estate, 19 Maiden Lane;* Walrus, *1906–08, formerly at 310 Sansome;* California Bear, *1936, Pioneer Hall, 456 McAllister Street.*

An Endangered Species

Time was when every edifice of size must have a lion or an eagle glowering from its street façade. The style was European and imperial—exactly what any ambitious American town aspired to be.

They are a dying breed, these totem animals, victims of changing fashion, construction costs, and safety regulations against overhanging cornices. Most of them were sculpted and installed in the first half of this century—between the '06 earthquake and the end of World War II—and in the past several decades few new sports have appeared.

Even in a hostile environment, however, a Darwinian principle applies. Earthbound mutations like Beniamino Bufano's *Penguins* in the Golden Gateway center animate the downtown streets. Crouching on granite pillows, skulking in niches of ivy among the glass cliffs, they have begun their struggle for survival. In defiance of the laws of evolution, a few doughty specimens—foxes, leopards, wolves, unicorns—cling to their imperiled ledges high above the busy crowd, but as these pictures were being taken, two more veterans succumbed.

49
PIONEER

We Know What We Like

More than any other civic ornament, a museum is a mark of political stability and established wealth. That explains why San Francisco, a fall-apart village on the rim of the earth, boasted of its first museum while most of the population was living in tents.

It wasn't exactly the Louvre—just a room at Robert B. Woodward's misleadingly named temperance hotel, the What Cheer House, containing six hundred stuffed birds, coins, eggs, seashells, pickled lizards, Indian weapons, and a four-legged chicken—but it was a start. In the 1870s Woodward was so far into culture that he opened a display of *paintings*. From there, it took merely a hundred years and a few hundred millions in private and public donations to develop four major, municipally sponsored art museums in the Bay Area: the de Young (Golden Gate Park), with its incomparable Avery Brundage Collection of Asian art; the Legion of Honor (Lincoln Park), in a neoclassic French palace on a bluff above the sea; the Museum of Art (Civic Center), with outstanding special exhibits and a respectable core of modern art; and the Oakland Museum, a three-in-one amalgam of history, science, and art in a brilliant modern building.

The art gallery at Woodward's Gardens in the 1870s (above) provided a velvet banquette from which to contemplate a hundred "old masters" copied by Californian Virgil Williams from European originals. One now can recline at the Oakland Museum (below), where emphasis is on the work of Western America—here, Toby Rosenthal's romantic extravagance The Trial of Constance de Beverley, *inspired by a Walter Scott novel.*

Sculpture is a major asset of the California Palace of the Legion of Honor, which owns more than forty works of Auguste Rodin, including one on the five original bronze casts of his renowned Thinker. *Important traveling exhibits regularly augment the Legion's collections of European and American painting, furniture, and graphics.*

Nucleus of the Bay Area's largest museum was the fine arts pavilion at the Midwinter Fair in Golden Gate Park in 1893–94 (above), a bit of old Egypt encrusted with hieroglyphs and stuffed with treasures from the attics of Nob Hill. M. H. de Young, director of the fair, persuaded the city to hang onto the building, then donated funds in 1917 for a larger gallery a few dozen yards west to replace it. Only a pair of wild-eyed sphinxes remain of the original spread, but the de Young Memorial Museum, several times remodeled and expanded, has become a national center of Asian and European art. Left: a docent shows visitors through a gallery of early Renaissance Italian masters; below, admirers study winning designs in a 1974 decorated denim contest.

The Pied Piper leads enchanted children over the hills and far away in retaliation for his ratty treatment by the burghers of Hamelin. The famous mural by Maxfield Parrish (1909) decorates a bar at the Sheraton Palace Hotel.

Wall-to-Wall Painting

Mural painting is an art that washes over cities in periodic waves. In Europe the currents usually are stirred up by monarchs, dictators, or political ideologies; here, by expositions, depressions, and attacks of conscience in large corporations.

The Panama-Pacific International Exposition of 1915 set off a ripple of frescoes and oil-on-canvas walls in the public buildings of San Francisco, but our tidal wave came with the Depression of the '30s, when the Federal Art Project of the Works Progress Administration, a New Deal work-relief program to employ needy artists, splashed the Bay Area with Art Deco sea life and protest of the Diego Rivera school.

We are riding another wave now: rainbow shoe stores, giant numerals, ethnic struggle. If you should see an empty wall, enjoy. It won't be blank for long.

Artist Lucien Labaudt (left) sketches the hand of park director John McLaren in wet plaster during a 1936–37 federal project at the Beach Chalet. The fresco portrays Labaudt's wife, fellow-artists, and students lolling amid landmarks of Golden Gate Park—the Conservatory, de Young Museum, Japanese Tea Garden.

Parnassus on the Pacific

As a fountain of literary inspiration, San Francisco has a constant but uneven flow. We house an impressive number of writers. Herbert Gold, a prolific writer himself, made a count some years ago and found about sixty "active novelists" working in the Bay Area, a selective census. But when one attempts to name those writers, past and present, who have dealt enduringly with northern California, the list becomes considerably shorter.

Many of our respected literary figures have lived here merely as sojourners, like expatriates in Mexico or Mallorca, drawing their material elsewhere, out of memory or imagination, as did Ambrose Bierce, the city's ferocious deacon of poetry and journalism in the 1880s, or Gelett Burgess, the whimsical balloon-popper of the '90s, or Allen Ginsberg, the poet, coming and going with other loosely mystical searchers in the 1950s.

On the other hand, those who have taken the region as a subject generally are known (if at all) as minor craftsmen with trivial themes: Gertrude Atherton, Charles Caldwell Dobie, Kathleen Norris, George Sterling, Stewart Edward White, Joaquin Miller . . . What the city always has provided is a vaguely literary ambiance: cheap cafes, fragile magazines, decrepit presses, warm bookshops, clusters of companionship to comfort writers in loneliness and soothe them in despair. In return for this indulgence, San Francisco has been rewarded by a few who have succeeded in telling the story of Western life: Bret Harte in his early gold rush tales; Mark Twain in *Roughing It;* Frank Norris in *McTeague;* Jack London in *Martin Eden;* William Saroyan in *The Time of Your Life;* John Steinbeck (never a San Franciscan but always a Californian) in *The Grapes of Wrath;* Wallace Stegner in his late novels; and two who left the West to interpret the lessons of California to the world—Josiah Royce in *California: From the Conquest in 1846 . . .* and Henry George in *Progress and Poverty.*

Top: "Blabbermouth Night" at The Place on upper Grant Avenue in 1957 afforded poets a platform and patrons a chance to act "Beat." Center: "Poppa" Coppa's Restaurant (Poppa at right) served full meals for fifty cents and permitted "Les Jeunes," the self-appointed Bohemians of the '90s, to paint walls with graffiti (e.g., "Paste Makes Waist") and names (their idols' and their own). Bottom: An all-male fandango at the Bohemian Club's grove on the Russian River around 1910 advertises the annual "Low Jinks" show.

A Sunday afternoon concert in the 1890s wafted from a plaster hemisphere in the southeast corner of Golden Gate Park (now the site of tennis courts), The figure 1 on the conductor's podium indicates the selection being played. In the distance: Electric Tower of the 1894 exposition.

The first music stand in the park (circa 1882) was an ivy-twined, arabesque gazebo with small-town charm and maddening acoustics. Later concerts grew more pretentious. The Municipal Band, dissolved in 1970, played to royal visitors and local commoners for fifty-eight years at the Music Concourse, a sunken oval seating twenty thousand.

There was dangling room only at Marx Meadow in Golden Gate Park for an alfresco rock concert by the People's Ballroom Collective in August 1974.

The Sound of Oompah

Rich as it is, the musical history of San Francisco cannot be conveyed in pictures. No woodcut recreates the homesick wail of fiddles in a gold rush saloon; no publicity portrait recaptures the sobbing tenor of Beniamino Gigli's *Andrea Chénier* at the first season of the San Francisco Opera in 1923; no on-stage snapshot rekindles the excitement of the San Francisco Ballet's first full-length *Nutcracker* (now an annual event) on Christmas eve, 1944.

There is an aspect of our musical heritage that photographers have captured, however, because it is one that depends as much on surroundings as sound—the outdoor concert. From the 1850s, when beer gardens first opened along the Mission Road, to the just-past decade of rock concerts in the park, we have shared the joy of music in the fine Pacific air.

A concert to benefit SNACK ("Students Need Athletics, Culture and Kicks") drew sixty thousand to Kezar Stadium in March 1975 to hear nine hours of Tower of Power, Santana, Doobie Brothers, Grateful Dead, Jefferson Starship, Neil Young, Joan Baez, Bob Dylan. Jugs like that at left (another concert) were prohibited.

A Little Street Music

It has been reported elsewhere (and far too often, in our opinion) that the great Italian soprano Luisa Tetrazzini drew two hundred thousand opera lovers to the corner of Kearny and Market Streets on Christmas Eve, 1910, to hear her sing "The Last Rose of Summer" and "Auld Lang Syne."

Good show, great audience, terrific boost for the old town—but if we are going to measure musical achievement like a sardine catch, who will ever have a word of praise for the late blind fiddler of Kearny Street, who entertained an uncountable audience in increments of, say, two or three around the turn of the century? Or for the one-man band of the Hyde Street turnaround, whose audience comes and goes by the cable-car load? Or the bearded bagpiper of Fisherman's Wharf, the trumpet-playing gorilla of Union Square, and the Embarcadero Plaza string quartet?

We who hurry past you, scattering few coins and sparse smiles, applaud you in our audience of millions—one at a time.

Stars of the fresh-air-and-sunshine circuit in recent appearances at (clockwise from upper right) Victorian Plaza, Market Street, the Sausalito ferry pier, and downtown Stockton Street.

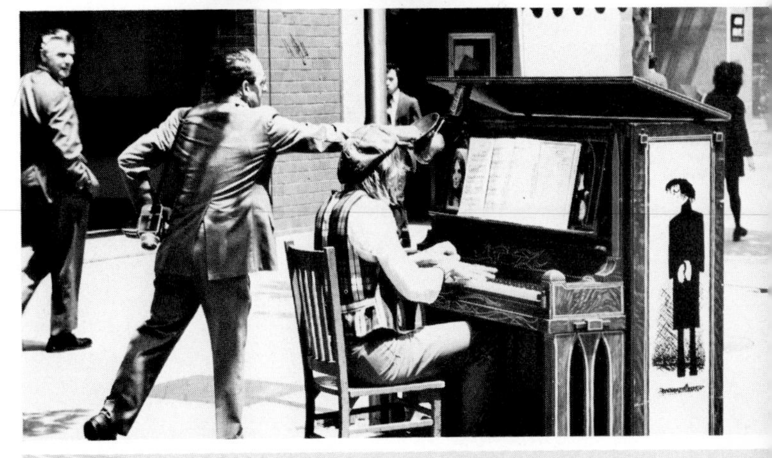

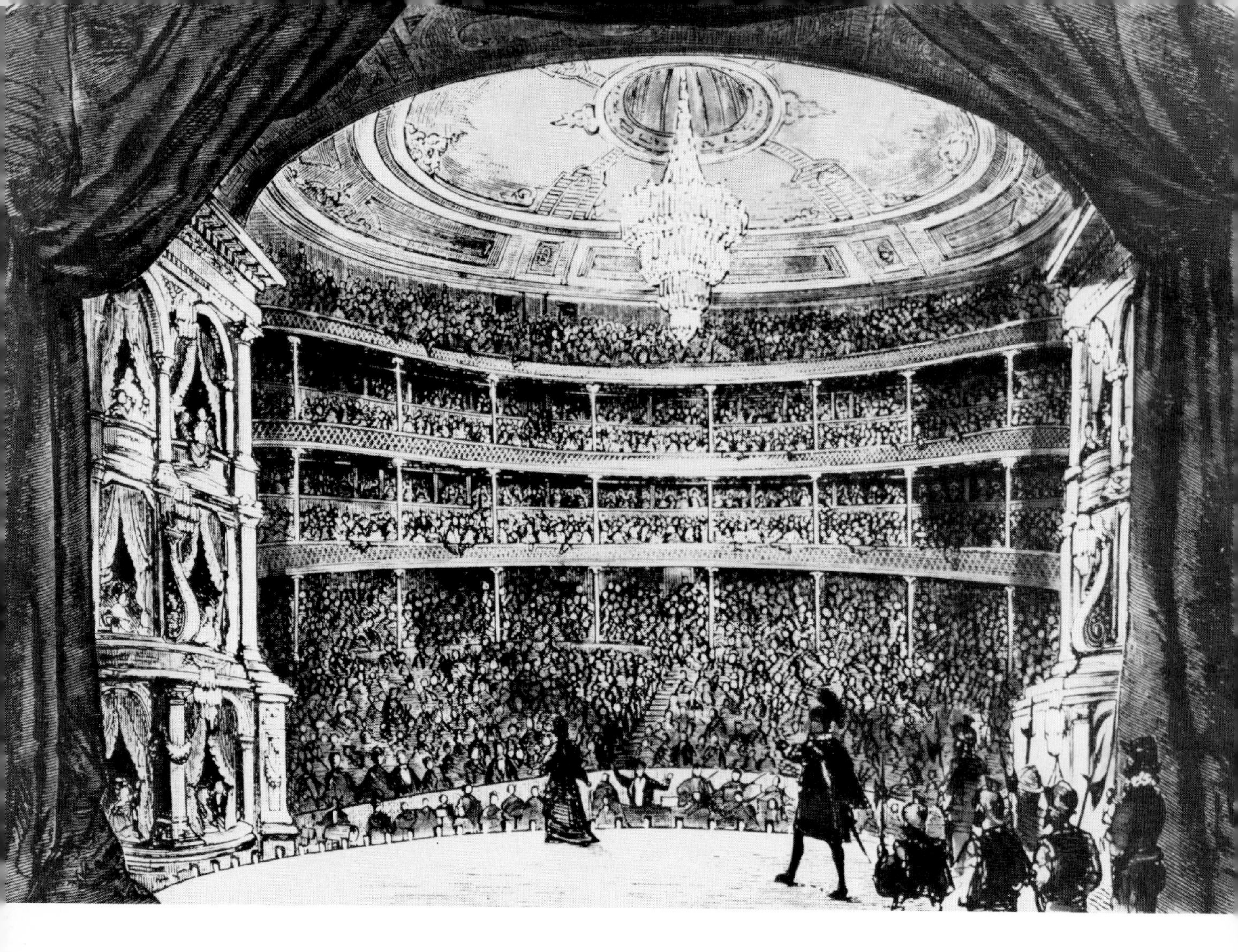

Grand Opera House on Mission Street near Third (above) offered melodramas, acrobats, Passion plays—even a few operas—from 1876 until its destruction in the 1906 fire. Enrico Caruso, who sang here in Carmen *the night before the disaster, fled the city and never returned, and a furniture store took over the site; but opera survived in music halls, auditoriums, and football stadiums. The grandiose municipal Opera House (below), a memorial to the dead of World War I, opened in 1932. Opera is now so popular that most of the 3,285 seats for each performance are sold before the season begins, and fanatics start lining up at midday for three hundred standing-room tickets.*

A Growing Crowd at the Porte-Cochere

Looking back on the crudity and irregularity of musical performances in San Francisco a century ago, one might assume that some sort of natural evolution has taken place, an inevitable growth of tiny seeds into an efflorescence of opera, symphony, and ballet. The autumn season of the San Francisco Opera, although shorter and less varied than that of New York, Milan, or Vienna, is now second to none in grandeur. The San Francisco Ballet, in its fifth decade, has developed the audience, repertoire, and reputation of a top American company. And the symphony, having endured a period of dissent and disintegration more than a dozen years ago, today forms the center post of musical culture in northern California.

None of this flowering was inevitable, of course: it was nurtured with love and fertilized with gold. The symphony was founded in 1912; the opera in 1923; the ballet (originally an adjunct to the opera) in 1933. The slow growth of each has been tended by a line of devoted directors: symphonic maestros Alfred Hertz, Pierre Monteux, Josef Krips, Seiji Ozawa, Edo de Waart; operatic maestros Gaetano Merola, the founding director, and Kurt Herbert Adler, his expansive successor; the brothers William, Harold, and Lew Christiansen of the ballet.

In evidence of its devotion to music, the city broke ground in 1978 for a $33.8 million performing arts center to include rehearsal rooms, an expanded Opera House, and a three-thousand-seat Symphony Hall, a considerable improvement on the Bella Union and the Mission Street Opera House.

A visit of Marietta Bonfanti of Milan's La Scala was typical of touring performances a hundred years ago. Her Pas de l'Ombre, *an interlude of classic ballet in a four-act drama called* Belphegor, the Montebank, *was followed by a Parisian virtuoso playing a newly invented horn, the saxophone.*

Tina Santos and Gary Wahl, doomed lovers in Michael Smuin's Shinju, *a world premiere by the San Francisco Ballet in 1975, stunned audiences with their erotic double hara-kari. After a season of writhing together, Santos and Wahl got married.*

Geary Street, dominated by road shows and repertory of the American Conservatory Theater (ACT), is the traditional theatrical district of the Bay Area but now shares audiences and talent with dozens of small playhouses scattered through many neighborhoods and suburbs.

The Limelight

It is presumptuous for a provincial city to rate itself "a good theater town," but San Francisco has been doing so, with its usual high level of self-esteem, since 1849, when Joseph Rowe's Olympic Circus set up at Clay and Kearny Streets and presented nine acrobatic equestrians and a prancing horse to a dazzled crowd of gold rush argonauts.

From that day on, according to innumerable books and articles, our theatrical history has been an unbroken succession of triumphs, from "Seeing the Elephant" (1850) at Robinson & Evrard's Dramatic Museum, where they painted the backdrop with mustard in lieu of chrome yellow; through the Actors' Workshop production of *Waiting for Godot,* which the Government exported to the World's Fair at Brussels in 1958; to the latest transubstantiation of Shaw by the American Conservatory Theater (ACT).

Lately, we even have experienced a little renaissance, a proliferation of earnest, undernourished repertory companies playing Brecht and Stoppard and Sophocles in church basements, lodge halls, and nightclubs.

Admittedly, we have seen a failure or two over the years. (Does anyone care to discuss the Spring Opera's *L'Amico Fritz,* the Civic Light Opera's *Wonderful Town,* or ACT's *Seagull?*) But the comforting thing about having a theatrical history is that one can counteract unpleasant memories by citing a performance no living person can recall. Did you, for example, see Adah Isaacs Menken ride bareback in *Mazeppa?* Did you see Lola Montez do her spider dance? Did you meet David Belasco? Do you remember Joe Murphy, singing in blackface with a County Kerry brogue, "A Handful of Earth from the Land of My Birth"? No? Don't speak to me of theater, my child.

Rosetta and Vivian Duncan, famous for Topsy and Eva, *a musical spoof of* Uncle Tom's Cabin, *led a line of touring cars up Eddy Street in the 1920s to tout a new review at the Tivoli. The Duncan Sisters outlived the theater, gutted for a garage in 1952.*

Where could a man of the 1860s find "songs, dances, recitations, imitations, beauty, wit, sentiment, good wines, cigars, brandy, and lager," all for two-bits admission? Where else but a melodeon, a masculine resort named for the dandy little pump organs that brought melody to gold rush saloons. Gilbert's, at Kearny and Clay Streets, was a paragon of this extinct species.

Tom Maguire's Opera House on Washington Street regaled entertainment-starved Westerners with concerts, circuses, burlesque, and Shakespeare from 1855 to 1873, making an ex-hackney driver from New York one of the richest, best-known showmen in America.

Movie palaces displaced legitimate theaters, here as elsewhere, then went into their own, TV-induced decay. The opening of the cavernous Fox Theater at Tenth and Market in June 1929 (right) capped a decade of extravagance. Less than thirty-five years later, the seats, mirrors, carpets, gilded box office, and giant pipe organ were auctioned off and the Fox was demolished. Porno flicks took over nightclubs, bars, even neighborhood movies in the 1960s, now are fading too.

City lights of three eras: Top, the incredible Electric Tower at the Midwinter Exposition (1894) beams its giant searchlight at the observatory on Strawberry Hill; right, the Ferry Building says hello and goodbye to the 1920s; left, the Transamerica Pyramid skewers the sky above Montgomery Street on a winter night in the 1970s.

Candlepower

Why do we come to the city at night, when the parking fees soar and the crime rate surges and the barkers at the topless joints on Broadway are bellowing, "Come on in—you're not too old to learn"?

Cities are unsafe and insalubrious—ours as much as most and more than many. Cities are expensive. Cities are inconvenient, uncomfortable, immoral, strenuous, fatiguing, impolite.

Most of us who swarm this dark and dangerous location have in mind a terminus—a cruising bar on Castro Street, a concert hall, an apartment with leather pillows in a corner and a pot of Swedish ivy hanging in the bay. But if the destination did not exist, we would invent one, a magnet to account for our unaccountable compulsion to congregate by night at the tip of this bumpy peninsula. Is it the bright lights that attract us, moth-like, to the city of our desires, the city that completes us and consumes our lives?

Acknowledgments

A book that attempts to picture two hundred years of physical and social change in an American city must depend upon impressions and mementos gathered by many persons and institutions. This book, more than most, has required the co-operation of friends whose names do not appear on the title page—researchers, photographers, librarians, collectors. The death of Paul C. Johnson in 1976, when the book was far from complete, put the burden of directing the project on two fine editors, Luther Nichols and Cathleen Jordan, and their patience and persistence have resulted in the completion of the work more or less the way Paul had planned it. In listing others who have been generous with time and materials, I undoubtedly will omit some who should be thanked. To those who have been neglected, I offer an apology and my appreciation for their unrewarded help, which Paul surely would have remembered and acknowledged.

RWR

Contributors of research, information, photographs, and invaluable personal assistance:

Marion Schulze, Suellen Bilow-Lerch, John Robinson, Hal Cruzan, Carl Poch, Caroline Crawford, Russell Thompson, Gladys Hansen, Richard Dillon, Ken Morino, Mrs. Lucien Labaudt, Palma Trentacoste, Hon. Finn Koren, Herman H. Beneke, Roger Olmsted, Judith L. Waldron, Charles Smallwood, Vernon J. Sappers, Chesley Bonestell, Lee Burtis, Jonathan Coleman, Eugene Sander, David Hartley, Louis Stein, Jr., Steve Tarantino, Alessandro Baccari, Chong Lee, Marilyn Bronson, Winston Elstob, Paul Ward, Ted Wurm, Albert Sperison, Ray Aker, Kenneth Cooperrider.

Business and labor organizations that provided pictures, background materials, and valued advice: Ghirardelli Square, The Cannery, North Point Pier, Hilton Hotel, Steam Beer Brewing Company, San Francisco Victoriana, Southern Pacific, Transamerica Corporation, Bank of America, Crown Zellerbach Corporation, American Airlines, Hyatt Regency Hotel, Golden Gate Fields, San Francisco 49ers, St. Francis Hotel, Prudential Lines, Sheraton Palace Hotel, Golden Hinde, Ltd., Fairmont Hotel, Mark Hopkins Hotel, Union Oil Company, San Francisco Giants, Matson Navigation Company, International Longshoremen's and Warehousemen's Union, Jack Tarr Hotel, Del Monte Corporation, L'Etoile Restaurant, Fior d'Italia Restaurant, I. Magnin, *San Francisco* magazine, Ammann & Whitney, San Francisco *Chronicle,* San Francisco *Examiner,* Furman Associates, Arnold & Palmer & Noble, *Sunset* magazine, *The Catholic Monitor.*

Libraries, museums, and archives: Society of California Pioneers, San Francisco Public Library (City Archives), Bancroft Library, Wells Fargo History Room, University of California Libraries, San Francisco Maritime Museum, M. H. de Young Museum, California Historical Society, Presidio Museum, San Francisco Archives for the Performing Arts, Oakland Museum, California State Library, Crocker Gallery (Sacramento), Library of Congress.

Promotional and cultural organizations: California State Automobile Association, Redwood Empire Association, San Francisco Convention & Visitors Bureau, Jackson Square Association, Market Street Development Association, Society for the Prevention of Cruelty to Animals, San Francisco Opera, San Francisco Ballet.

Departments of the San Francisco city and county government: Recreation and Park Department, Port Commission, Municipal Railway, Art Commission, Redevelopment Agency, Department of City Planning, Department of Public Works, Fire Department, International Airport, George Peabody School, Mission High School.

Other agencies of government: Bay Area Rapid Transit District; Golden Gate Bridge and Transportation Authority; State Department of Transportation (CalTrans); Royal Norwegian Consulate General, San Francisco; Alameda-Contra Costa Transit; Port of Oakland.

Sorter, arranger, selector, and rejector of countless pictures and layout designer of innumerable picture spreads: John Beyer.

Helpmeet and comforter: Joan Reinhardt

Picture Credits

Many persons and institutions kindly have given us permission to use photographs, which are identified here by page and by position (t—top; c—center; b—bottom; l—left; r—right). A key to the abbreviations appears at the end of these picture credits.

Front matter: 1—S B-L; 2—ReinCol; 3—Russ Thompson/Manta Products; 4—Ban; 5—RWR; 6—WF; 7—S B-L; 8—W. E. Worden WF; 9—Hyatt Regency; 10—Ban; 11—RWR; 12—Ban; 13—RWR.

Chapter 1: 14—(t) SFPL, (b) Robert Cameron; 15—EF; 16—(t) Ban, (b) John Robinson; 17—(t) NP, (c) SFPL, (b) Marion Schulze; 18—(t) WF, (bl), MB, (br) S B-L; 19—(t) KR, (bl) Smallwood, (br) KR; 20—(t) RRO, (c) Ban, (b) RWR; 21—(tl) Ban, (tr, bl) KR, (br) S B-L; 22—(t) WF, (b) RWR; 23—(t) WF, (b) NP; 24—(tl) Ban, (tr) RWR, (b) SFPL; 25—(tl) CSL, (tr) RWR, (bl) CHS, (c) Ban, (br) Bank of America; 26—(t)SFPL, (b) ReinCol; 27—(t) KR, (bl) SFPL, (br) ReinCol; 28—(cl) SFPL, (bl) Bank of America, (r) Gerald Frederick; 29—(tl) ReinCol, (tr, bl) SFPL, (br) KR; 30—(tr, cl) Ban, (b) E. B. Crocker Art Gallery, Sacramento; 31—(t) S B-L, (bl) SF Redevelopment Agency, (br) KR; 32—(t) WF, (bl) CHS, (br) CP; 33—(t, br) KR, (bl) S B-L; 34—(t) SFPL, (b) KR; 35—(tl) KR, others (3) SFPL; 36—WF; 37—(bl) RWR, (tr) SFPL, (br) KR; 38—(br) SoCalPio, others (3) SFPL; 39—(t) PMR, (b) KR(2).

Chapter 2: 41—Gary Fong/SF *Chronicle;* 42—(t) LoC, (c) Hal Cruzan, (b) RWR; 43—(c) LoC, (b) SF Port Commission; 44—(t) Ban, (b) S B-L; 45—(bl) KR, (br) SF *Examiner;* 46—(b) RWR; 47—(t) KR, (map) PCJ; 48—(t) SFPL, (b) EF; 49—(c, bl) NP, (br) KR; 50—(t) Ban, (b) LoC; 51—(t) RWR, (bl) KR, (br) S B-L; 52—(b) S B-L; 53—(t, b) RWR, (c) S B-L; 54—(t) Smallwood, (b) William Bronson; 55—(tl) KR, (tr) S B-L, (b) Ban; 56—(t) SP, (b) Golden Gate Transit; 57—(c) S B-L, (b) SP; 58—(t) SP, (b) KR; 59—(tl, b) S B-L, (tr, c) SP.

Chapter 3: 60—PMR; 61—SFPL; 62—(t) SFPL, (b) CHS; 63—(t & bl) RWR, (c) CHS, (br) Ban; 64—(t) SFPL, (b) KR; 65—(t & b) S B-L, (c) KR; 66—CNS (2); 67—(t) KR, (bl) CHS, (br) NP; 68—(t) Ban, (c) CHS, (b) WF; 69—(t, bl) KR, (bc, r) S B-L; 70—(t) CHS, (b) MB; 71—(tl) Tom Tracy; (bl, br) EF, (cr) Hal Cruzan, (cb) RWR; 72—(t) SFPL, (b) RWR; 73—(t, bl) SFPL, (c) RWR, (br) KR; 74—(t) WF, (b) SFPL; 75—(t, c) SFPL, (b) KR (2); 76—(t) © Robert A. Isaacs, 1968, (b) KR (2); 77—JohnCol.

Chapter 4: 78—(t) Paul Ward, (b) RWR; 79—S B-L; 80—JohnCol (2); 81—(t, c) Smallwood, (b) KR; 82—(t) Smallwood, (b) Ban; 83—(t) KR, (bl) MB, (br) Smallwood; 84—S B-L; 85—(t) SF Municipal Railway, (c) KR; 86—(t) S B-L, (b) MB; 87—(t) MB, (cl, r) S B-L, (br) American Airlines photo by Bob Takis; 88—(t) Smallwood, (b) KR; 89—(t, bl) Paul Ward, (br) SFPL; 90—CSAA (2); 91—(t, bl) CSAA, (c) KR, (br) RWR; 92—ConVisBur; 93—(t) Ted Wurm, (b) NP; 94—(t) SF *Examiner,* (b) RWR; 95—(t) CHS, (bl) Ban, (br) ConVisBur; 96—A/C Transit, Oakland, Cal. (3); 97—(t, c) San Francisco Bay Area Rapid Transit District, (bl) SP, (br) S B-L; 98—(t) Ban, (c) State Department of Transportation, (b) RWR; 99—(t) Golden Gate Bridge & Transit District, (b) KR; 100—(t) SFPL, (b) SFO; 101—(t, c) SFPL, (b) SFO.

Chapter 5: 102—EF; 103—(l) Tim Johnson, (r) Ban; 104—(t) WF, (b) RWR; 105—(t) CSL, (c, bl) KR, (br) CHS; 106—(t) CHS, (b) Ban; 107—(t) NP, (c) RRO, (b) KR (2); 108—ConVisBur (2); 109—(tl, b) Ban, (cl) LoC, (tr) PMR; 110—(t) Ban, (b) CHS (3); 111—ConVisBur (3); 112—(t) Lee Burtis, (c, b) John Col; 113—(t) KR, (bl) ConVisBur, (br) NP; 114—(t) KR, (bl) EF, (br) Steve Tarantino; 115—(t) S B-L, (c) Sutro Library, San Francisco, (b) Eureka Federal Savings North Beach Museum; 116—(t) Ban, (bl) CSL, (br) SFPL; 117—(t, c) S B-L, (b) NP; 118—(t, bl) SFPL, (tr) Air News Photo, San Francisco; 119—(t) Ban (b) SFPL; 120—(t) CSL, (b) RWR; 121—(t, br) SFPL, (bl) RWR; 122—S B-L; 123—(cl) KR, (cr, br) S B-L, (bl) San Francisco Ballet.

Chapter 6: 124—SFPL (4); 125—RWR; 126—PCJ, (bl) Ban, (br) Drake Navigators Guild; 127—(t) PCJ, (b) NP; 128—(t) Ban, (b) Winston Elstob, Nov. 30, 1975, Yuma, Ariz.; 129—KR (2); 130—(t) SoCalPio, (b) ReinCol; 131—(t) RWR, (b) JohnCol; 132—(t) Presidio Army Museum Coll., Presidio of San Francisco, (c) Ban, (b) MB; 133—(t) KR (4), (b) S B-L; 134—(t) CHS, (b) KR; 135—(t, bl) RWR; (br) CHS; 136—(t) Ban, (b) Presidio Army Museum Coll. (2); 137—(t) KR, (b) S B-L (2); 138—(t) MB (c, b) CHS; 139—(t) RWR, (b) SFPL; 140—(t) Old Mint Museum, San Francisco, (b) RWR; 141—(t) PCJ, (c) S B-L, (b) SoCalPio; 142—KR; 143—(t) CP, (b) Ban; 144—(t) CP, (b) WF; 145—(t, c) KR, (b) S B-L; 146—LoC; 147—(1) CHS, (r) S B-L.

Chapter 7: 148—Jeremiah O. Bragstad; 149—S B-L (2); 150—(t) Ban, (b) RWR; 151—(t) WF, (b) PMR (2); 152—(t) Ban, (b) The Cannery; 153—PMR; 154—(t) S B-L, (b) MB (2); 155—(tl) San Francisco Victoriana, (tr) PCJ, others (2); 156—(t) MB, (b) RWR; 157—(t, cr) MB, (cl) Craig Zwicky, (b) ReinCol; 158—(t) CHS, (bl) S B-L, (br) WF; 159—S B-L (2); 160—(t) JohnCol (2), (bl) Ban, (br) SFPL; 161—(t) CSL, (b) RWR (2); 162—(t) SFPL, (b) RWR; 163—SFPL (3); 165—(t) RWR, others (2) S B-L; 166—CHS; 167—(t, br) S B-L, (bl) CHS; 168—(t) Ban, (b) *The Monitor,* the official paper of the Archdiocese of San Francisco. (2); 169—(tl) SF Fire Department, others (3) *The Monitor;* 170—(t) LoC, (b) Ban; 171—(t, c) RWR, (b) CP.

Chapter 8: 172—(t) Ban, (b) NP; 173—EF; 174—(c, bl) S B-L, (br) MB; 175—(t) Ban, (bl) KR, (bc) Lee Foster, (br) Lee Burtis; 176—(t) Ban, (bl) MB, (br) KR; 177—(t) RWR, (c) MB, (b) KR; 178—(tl, b) CP, (tr) RWR; 179—(t) CP, (b) RRO; 180—(t) SFPL, (bl) JohnCol, (br) S B-L; 181—MB (3); 182—(tl) SFPL, (tr) KR, (b) Ban; 183—(t) NP, (bl) KR, (br) Gary Fong/SF *Chronicle;* 184—(br) CP, (bl) S B-L; 185—(t) CP, (c, bl) S B-L, (br) EF; 186—(t) MB, (b) Ban; 187—S B-L (2); 188—(bl) S B-L; 189—(t) CHS, (bl) Ban, (br) S B-L; 190—(t) MB, (c) CHS (2); 191—(t) Baron Wolman, (c) Gerald Frederick, (b) S B-L; 192—(t) Ban, (b) SF Giants; 193—(t, b) SF 49ers, (c) Ban; 194—SF Giants (2); 195—(t, c) Ban, (b) SFPL; 196—(t) Ban, (b) SF *Examiner;* 197—(t) Chong Lee, (bl, br) © Chronicle Publishing Co., (bc) Wide World; 198—(t) Diane Beeston, (b) Ban; 199—(t) RRO, (b) Diane Beeston; 200—(t) WF, (b) CSL; 201—Golden Gate Fields, Albany, Calif. (4).

Chapter 9: 202—CHS; 203—(1) EF, (r) NP; 204—(t) S B-L, (b) ReinCol; 205—(t) SoCalPio, (b) SFPL; 206—(t, c) SFPL, (b) S B-L; 207—(t) EF, (b) SFPL; 208—(t, bl) SFPL, (br) S B-L; 209—(t, bl) MB, (cr) ReinCol, (br) SFPL, (bl) MB; 210—NP; 211—(tl) JohnCol. (tr) MB, (b) SFPL; 212—(t) Gary Fong/SF *Chronicle,* (b) RWR; 213—(t) Ban, (b) SFPL; 214—(t) KR, (b) ReinCol; 215—(t, b) Anchor Brewing Company, (c) SFPL.

Chapter 10: 216—CHS, (r) S B-L; 217—S B-L; 218—S B-L; 219—S B-L (6); 220—(t) RRO, (b) NP; 221—(tr) WF, others (3) NP; 222—(t) Sheraton-Palace Hotel, (b) Mrs. Lucien Labaudt (2); 223—S B-L (2); 224—(t) Dan Tooker, (b) ReinCol; 225—(t, c) SFPL, (b) Ban; 226—(t) CP, (b) MB; 227—(t) S B-L, (bl) NP, (br) © Michael Zagaris; 228—Ban; 229—(bl) KR, others (3) S B-L; 230—(t) Collections of the SF Archives for the Performing Arts, (b) SF Opera Asssociation; 231—(t) Caroline Crawford, (c) Collections of the SF Archives for the Performing Arts, (b) Arne Folkedal/SF Ballet; 232—(t) NP, (b) SFPL; 233—(tl) RRO, (tr) Ban, (bl) EF, (br) SFPL; 234—NP; 235—(t) WF, (b) CHS; 236—JohnCol; 237—S B-L.

KEY

Ban: Bancroft Library, University of California, Berkeley; ConVisBur: San Francisco Convention and Visitors Bureau; CHS: California Historical Society; CP: Carl Poch, San Francisco Recreation and Park Department; CSAA: California State Automobile Association; CSL: California Section, California State Library, Sacramento; EF: Ellen Fernandez; JohnCol: Paul Johnson Picture Collection; KR: Kurt A. Reinhardt; LoC: Library of Congress; MB: Marilyn Blaisdell Collection; NP: Norman Prince; PCJ: Paul C. Johnson; PMR: Paul M. Reinhardt; ReinCol: Richard Reinhardt Picture Collection; RRO: Roger Olmsted Picture Collection; RWR: Richard Reinhardt; S B-L: Suellen Bilow-Lerch; SFO: Public Relations Officer, San Francisco Internal Airport; SFPL: City Archives, San Francisco Public Library; Smallwood: Charles Smallwood Picture Collection; SoCalPio: Society of California Pioneers; SP: Southern Pacific Transportation Company; WF: Wells Fargo Bank History Room, San Francisco.

Index